QUAY VOICES

#3

NEW WRITING

FROM QUAY WORDS

EXETER CUSTOM HOUSE

2022-2023

Edited by Heather Norman-Soderlind,
Trustee, Literature Works

Quay Words

CONTENTS

PUBLISHER'S NOTE

Quay Words is a non-profit programme, showcasing literature as an accessible and diverse art form. It offers concessions and bursaries to increase access for all. Proceeds from the sale of this anthology will be invested into the programme, allowing Quay Words to continue supporting inclusive access to literature, writing and stories at Exeter Custom House.

www.quaywords.org.uk

INTRODUCTION

HELEN CHALONER
CHIEF EXECUTIVE, LITERATURE WORKS

Quay Words 2022–2023 was our fifth year of presenting a varied, lively and inclusive programme of live literature at Exeter Custom House: an iconic building in a UNESCO City of Literature. After extensive consultations with partners and communities, we launched our pilot season in the summer of 2019, aimed at animating a truly stunning building with no previous record as a cultural venue. From a standing start, and with a pandemic intervening, we are proud of what Quay Words has achieved. The small Literature Works teams programmes and delivers Quay Words on behalf of Exeter Canal and Quay Trust, and we are immensely grateful for their sustained support. We also thank Arts Council England, a core funder of Literature Works and generous supporter of the programme. During the year, we continued building a range of wonderfully fruitful partnerships with, amongst others, the University of Exeter, the Wellcome Centre for Cultures and Environments of Health, Honeyscribe, Libraries Unlimited, the Devon & Exeter Institution, Speaking Volumes Live Literature

Productions, Resilient Women and Co-Lab, Little Toller Books, Headway Devon, and RAMM (Royal Albert Memorial Museum). We have enjoyed collaborating with them all.

Quay Voices #3 – New Writing from Quay Words at Exeter Custom House – is the third in our series, following on from *Quay Voices #1* (Impress Books, 2021) and *Quay Voices #2* (Literature Works, 2022). Covering the period from spring 2022 through to the summer of 2023, the anthology presents the contributions of wide and varied voices. As with the two previous anthologies, *Quay Voices #3* showcases the work of emerging writers who took part in the programme alongside the established authors with whom they worked at Quay Words. Excerpts from the works of writers who led residencies, courses, workshops and mentoring in the programme sit next to the new writing that these writers helped to nurture. We believe this makes for a deliciously readable and enjoyable collection which is truly representative of the programme. Not forgetting, of course, the free activities that took place inside and in front of the building, aimed at enticing people in for more – ranging from the Poetry Machine to Storytelling with Clive PiG – which have all been great fun.

Quay Words runs throughout the year, with three themed seasons of particularly intense activity. This year's season themes were 'Maritime', to complement the first Maritime Heritage Festival on the Quay; 'Heritage', which connected Quay Words to the 1,000-year literary history of Exeter; and 'Threads' which linked to Exeter's past wool-making and dyeing trade. A highlight was Andrew Miller's 'Hothouse', a three-day intensive writing experience for selected writers. We are delighted to share the work of two such writers who joined Andrew in April 2023, alongside an excerpt from Andrew's latest novel *The Slowworm's Song*.

Next-generation writers are not forgotten. Quay Words' annual invitation for young people aged 8–18 to submit a piece of flash fiction on the subject of 'Trading Places' saw a record number of entries of high quality. We are delighted to share the winning entries as our *Young Voices* in this volume.

Over 4,250 people have attended and actively participated in person since Quay Words first opened its doors. A total of 160 writers have been part of he programme to date, including 15 writers-in-residence. A huge thanks to all of them and to our many essential partners whom we acknowledge at the back of the book. We thank all our writers, established and new, who took part in workshops and classes, and we thank all who bought tickets to be part of the Quay Words community, in person or online, throughout this year.

GRETA STODDART

GUEST WRITER, OCTOBER 2022

Greta Stoddart studied drama at Manchester University and acting at the École Internationale de Théâtre Jacques Lecoq in Paris. She co-founded the theatre company Brouhaha. Her first poetry collection, *At Home in the Dark* (Anvil Press, 2001), won the Geoffrey Faber Memorial Prize and was shortlisted for the Forward Prize for Best First Collection. Her second, *Salvation Jane* (Anvil, 2008), was shortlisted for the Costa Poetry Award. In 2007 she was nominated by *Mslexia* as one of the best ten contemporary women poets in the UK. Her third collection, *Alive Alive O* (Bloodaxe Books, 2015) was shortlisted for the Roehampton Poetry Prize. Her radio drama *Who's There?*, broadcast on Radio 4's *The Echo Chamber* in 2017, was shortlisted for the Ted Hughes Award. Her fourth collection, *Fool*, was published by Bloodaxe in 2022.

Greta lives in Devon and teaches seminars for the Poetry School in Exeter, Axminster and Bridport.

Performance

GRETA STODDART

I'm sitting at an open window
in a new light
wondering why it is
that when I write
I sometimes seem to know
more than I actually do –
some fool out there
keeps falling down and getting up
and trying hard
to make me laugh
but I want to stay inside
and ask myself
if this is true.
Because I don't feel I know
very much at all
but my poems – look at them
waving their inky little hands in the air!
Watch me take a word,
a single word
like defenestration
and consider it
in a cold structural way
which is to say
without thinking of a body

throwing itself out of a window
for what's lodged deep inside it
to make its great escape.
There I go again.
Please understand
that is not what I want
for the body – I want it to land,
brush itself down and keep
on with the show.

From *Fool*, Greta Stoddart,
Bloodaxe Books, 2022,
reprinted with permission.

ALICE ALBINIA

WRITER-IN-RESIDENCE, OCTOBER 2022

Alice Albinia is the award-winning author of twinned works of fiction and non-fiction. Her first two books explore overlapping cultural and geographical territory in Pakistan, India, Afghanistan and Tibet. *Empires of the Indus: The Story of a River*, published in 2008, won six prizes in Britain, Pakistan, France and Italy. *Leela's Book*, published in 2011, was longlisted for the DSC Prize for South Asian Literature and shortlisted for the Authors' Club Best First Novel Award.

Her two new books are about Britain and its islands. *The Britannias*, a portrait of Britain which knocks the centre out, was published by Penguin, 2023. Her new novel, *Cwen*, set on an archipelago off the east coast of Britain which comes under female rule, out now with Serpent's Tail, was shortlisted for the Orwell Prize for Political Fiction.

She previously worked as an editor and journalist in Delhi, teaches and lectures in universities and schools, and has travelled all around Britain, piecing together ancient, medieval and modern myths of islands ruled by women.

During her residency at Quay Words, she took her first steps into a new literary project about Exeter's connection via nineteenth-century trade to Peru, within – as she commented – 'the very Custom House where some of those troubling and exciting stories began'.

Of those writers who joined Alice during her workshop on Narrative Non-Fiction and submitted work to us subsequently, Alice has selected Juan Carlos Mendez, Cherry Bedford and Abby Crawford as *Quay Voices*.

Bird Song

ALICE ALBINIA

'Mis Ane Bishop la Sirena de Albion.'
El Comercio, Lima, Peru, 31st October 1857

Anna knew that Maria Phelan's plan was gnarly. It meant travelling from Peru to Bristol, where Anna had a concert, in a new hall. It meant scandalising local society by finding Maria's father. It meant contacting journalists to spread the warning that the wonder drug being imported to England would haunt it like a Quechuan curse. It meant avenging herself on those same British merchants whose guano business had killed her brother.

Nevertheless, even as she listened, out at sea, sipping her cocktail, Anna felt her serenity returning. Everything about that month in Lima had been good – the seabirds, the song, the seven concerts, above all Maria herself. Lima was a harbinger. Anna had run for her life through the past twenty years and it was only in Lima that she stopped to catch her breath.

She shut her eyes and thought – of her daughter, in England, yes; of the scandalous flight from the first husband, with the second, indeed; of the wild journeys she and her reprobate harpist lover had made through Denmark, Sweden and Russia – but she thought mostly of Maria herself. They had met in that city, Lima, with its aristocrats dressed in silks brought from Paris, wearing thin black scarves which fell from their heads, revealing feathers in their hair and jewels on their necks. Diamonds sparkled on their fingers and wrists. Anna had loved the creak of the stage at the Teatro Principal; the cries of *Bravo*! and *Otra*! and *Maravillosa*!; the taste on her tongue of the cocktail they created for her, *La Sirena*, with lime, sugar, Pisco and a sprinkling of sacred cinnamon. The smell as she stepped outside the theatre afterwards: sea salt and heavy grey clouds.

She held an image in her mind: Maria, during that first concert in Lima, waiting in the wings. Her newly appointed maid had been wearing a green dress and the ubiquitous black veil. Anna had been dressed up in flowery local embroidery for the pigeon song. The audience was roaring its approval. As she turned to come off stage, Anna's eyes met Maria's.

She saw somebody younger than her, and wiser. She remembered the rush of peace.

What Maria felt and saw, specifically, Anna was only just discovering now, on the boat to Chile.

When Anna first met Maria, both her first husbands were dead. She had left the so-called second (the first had refused to divorce her), interred outside Sydney, his grave marked with a white marble edifice of a woman kneeling before a harp. The man who was to become husband number three, Martin Schultz, was already by her side, having travelled with them on the hellish nine-week boat journey from San Francisco, where he had been prospecting, to Sydney, where, within weeks, he was following in the sixth of Bochsa's twenty-carriage cortège.

The news of the Indian Mutiny had reached Anna when she was still in Sydney, at Bochsa's deathbed. India was unknown to her, a country she hadn't yet toured. But she had an acquaintance in Cawnpore, and a blood relative in Delhi. She felt shock and horror, as her eyes ran over the headlines.

In mid-September, as her party left Sydney, the latest information was that innocent British women and children were being slaughtered by the dozen. She felt scandalised by the thought of an Indian soldier rising up and killing her cousin George. Anna could feel the distress of it, pricking her eyelids and making her fingers fidget, all the way to Callao. She sat on deck, staring out at the ocean. Sometimes, she didn't move from her chair for hours. As she stared out at the salty water, day after day, her head felt fuzzy. She felt sick at the thought of opening her throat to sing.

She heard the birds above her the moment she came on deck, that last morning at sea. There they were: cawing and whirling through the sky. Her fingers gripped the handrail of the first class deck; she arched her neck and listened. What a noise they made! As operas went, the cacophony was intense: busy, self-important, unforgettable. She closed her eyes and let the bird calls fill her senses. Oh, to be a bird.

Then they came within sight of land. Anna stood, pressed against the rail, as the country took shape through the mist. The city which was their destination stood and waited for them at the top of a cliff.

Anna found Maria on the second night in Lima. Her first concert was in five days' time. She needed two things, as always: a local costume and a local song. It had always worked like a tonic in the past.

The manager of the theatre sent her Maria Phelan. He explained, somewhat elaborately, that Maria was a *Mestiza*, the product of an Indian woman and the Irish overseer of the guano mines near Pisco. An Indian woman? For one moment Anna thought he was referring to the mutiny in Delhi. He coughed, and explained that the woman was local, indigenous. He repeated the word in Spanish, *indígena*, as if to reassure himself.

Well, Anna didn't care where Maria came from, or how; only that she should arrive with a song.

The woman who called herself Maria Phelan was shorter than Anna, and darker. Impossible to age. She had long, black hair that shone. The song she offered Anna was in Quechua, from the highlands of Ayacucho; her people had brought it down with them when they came to work in the mines. Anna learnt the words carefully. *Hina ripuchan, hina pasachun chay urpi.*

Let my pigeon fly; only then will she remember my love.

She will pay for my tears, crying like a river, like the rain.

A song in Spanish would be better, the manager of the theatre warned. But Anna thought otherwise. She had sung of Vikings to the scholars of Uppsala University; in Russian to the Tsar; *La Catatumba* in Mexico, while wearing a sombrero. Of course, she would run through the arias by Bellini, Rossini, even Verdi, irritating though he was. But when she brought the house down, it would be with a Peruvian song from the hills, sung, Norma-like, by a spurned and angry lover.

Maria taught her to sing it in a morning. Afterwards, Anna ordered lunch for them both, and they ate it sitting on the veranda of the hotel, as mists from the sea wreathed everything they could see, except each other. Anna praised the fruit, *mango*, which she had never tasted before, and explained to Maria about her need for a local costume. Maria explained, in her turn, that the aristocratic women of Peru never wore local cloth. But she knew a tailor who could embellish any blouse and skirt with panels of embroidery and weaving.

'You could also strum a *charango*,' Maria said, 'and wear a hat.'

Anna laughed. She was forty-seven. She had toured

Europe in her twenties; America and Australia in her thirties. Before her disgrace, she had sung at the coronation of Queen Victoria; after it, for Europe's royalty. In Naples, where she was prima donna, King Ferdinand of the Two Sicilies had been her patron. From one end of the world to the other, she had entertained nobles and commoners, ambassadors and bandits. She had seen everything.

It was December when they set off for Chile. Anna observed Maria, out on deck, watching as her land slid away before her eyes. Halfway through the journey, they passed some tall islands not far from the coast, white with bird shit.

'The guano,' Maria said; and later, Schultz confirmed it: 'Where her father worked. They bring labourers from China. Indians won't do it anymore.'

Schultz knew all about mining. He had tried to invest in the guano, but the global monopoly was with a British firm. Instead, he had bought shares in Peruvian silver. They were still extracting the ore, even though the heyday had been 200 years before. His eyes glittered as he described to Anna how common silver once was, in Peru. During the height of the silver rush, in the seventeenth century, even the peasants ate off silver plates. Lima was paved in silver for the Viceroyalty's procession.

Out on deck, Anna ordered another *La Sirena*.

She wished she had been taken to see Maria's

family before they left Lima. But Maria had only introduced her to the tailor, a woman with deft fingers, who had altered her costume for the pigeon song, in a rundown part of town where the one-storey houses were seemingly made from mud, on streets that stank of shit. Maria's father had left for Britain a year before and nobody spoke of her mother. Her brother had been killed in an accident, the theatre manager said, out on those islands where the guano was mined.

Anna watched Maria crossing the deck towards her. Only as their eyes sought each other did she realise what she hadn't in Lima: that the tailor and the mother were one and the same.

The boat's siren sounded – long, deep – and Anna's body began to shake at the thought of everything the woman had kept hidden in her heart.

When Maria sat down beside her, and began to speak, quietly in her ear, Anna could feel the warmth of her breath, the passion in her plan. She was laying it out, very clearly, everything she needed to do.

Anna held Maria's hand, which was shaking too. She sipped her drink and watched a bird, a pelican, flying over the boat, and away to the horizon. Together, they watched its powerful wings beating the air, its black body and huge white beak. They listened for its call, but could hear nothing over the noise of the boat.

Anna said, 'It is carrying the message ahead of us to England.'

Maria said, 'My brother's journey has begun.'

Yes, it was gnarly. But Anna saw that it was necessary, too. She nodded her assent.

Musical Landscapes

JUAN CARLOS MENDEZ

Sleeping while someone else drives is always discourteous. However, the responsibility of staying awake decreases if several passengers are in the car; in this case, a strategy game emerges: the first one to go to sleep is free from any guilt and will even receive a tender gaze – as if they were a child. On the contrary, it's understood that the last one to stay awake shall remain in this state for the rest of the trip. Normally, this should be the co-pilot, but I don't give Ramon more than five minutes of wakefulness. I had better start thinking of something to say to Rich.

To make matters worse, the radio is playing *Jupiter* – they really love this *planet* at Classic FM. It's a sweet piece of course, and I would surely get goose bumps if I were to hear *I Vow to Thee My Country* live, even if I'm Mexican, even if patriotic symbols give me an itch – whether they are from my homeland or not. An exception to this last point would be the *Ode to Joy*; Europeans have made it their hymn, sure, but I would say that, in reality, it is humankind's hymn, however sentimental this might sound.

But coming back to where we were – that is, to *Jupiter* – played like this, as an orchestral planet and not as a choral hymn, on this old car radio that can hardly pick up two radio stations, and added to the fatigue that has come after two days of rock climbing, it will end up lulling us all, including Rich, who's been driving since we left the Isle of Portland. I would not rule out that some of the car accidents one sees on the M5 are due in part to Classic FM's insistence on playing this heavenly work. What an irony that the only other option that this radio picks up is so full of American pop. How is it possible that Pink Floyd, Portishead, Radiohead, Amy Winehouse, and a very long etcetera have come from this island?

The landscapes, though, match the music to perfection: they follow one after another as a series of postcards or calendar pictures. Variations on a single theme: idyllic green hills dotted with cottony white sheep, geometrical wooden barns and stables that pop up from a children's book, orange hay bales mirroring the summer clouds, a cosy countryside cottage, *Sunday roast served until 6pm*. I hope we stop for dinner soon. But just as I'm about to propose it – seizing the fact that *Jupiter* has finally faded out – as my tongue prepares to ask if anyone else is hungry, the chords of a guitar, unmistakable from the first one, stop me. For a moment, realising we are about to start listening to another piece with lulling potential, I think of opening a window or pushing the gastro poll (would you vote for a pizza place or a pub?) but the three notes of the

English horn stop me again. The same has happened to the rest of the crew: their thoughts have ceased wandering – I can sense it somehow – their attention has come back inside this car that keeps cutting through the hot humid summer air. Even Rich seems to slow down, precluding the engine from obscuring the adagio from the *Concierto de Aranjuez*.

The music still matches the landscape, though the evocative dry air that comes out of the guitar no longer fits as well with the fresh little hills. It now goes better with something that is not outside but inside: Lucia and Ramon – they were both born in the same land as this music. Yet why do I feel as if this guitar were Mexican too? Is it because it is the instrument of mariachis and ballad players? Is it because, placed side by side with pale white skins, the sun-roasted hues of Spaniards and mine suddenly seem akin? Us Mexicans could be the jack of all trades of nationalities: so many times, while trying to guess where I'm from, people have guessed the entire world (this is an exaggeration, no one has thought me Korean or Japanese). Nevertheless, once challenged, most have chosen Spanish as their first guess. And this is even after having heard me speak; in tongues, as in skin tones, subtleties in accents go unnoticed when different languages and nationalities are compared.

It is to be expected; no matter how much we insist on reminding ourselves that the Spanish conquered *us*, in my case, in the raffle of father- and motherlands, rather than being born amongst the conquered or conquerors (perennial groups in Mexico), I got to be mixed race, a textbook Mexican, half-brother of Lucia and Ramon. And this nuance in the consanguinity, here, in England, loses its relevance. Whether we say *tío*, or *güey*, we Spanish speakers are foreigners here, immigrants who long for the same mother tongue. We share the same nostalgia that turns into a fraternising force as powerful as entrusting your life to the human on the other side of the climbing rope. We know it, we are not from around here, the children's book landscapes and the mild weather yell it to us. We are reminded by the nervous greetings, the parties with music but solitary dancing – glass in hand – boiled veggies and a Yorkshire pudding, thick gravy trickling from them (in the end we decided to stop at a pub in Sidford).

Lacking great weather, the English have become experts at creating cosy interiors. Ales have been spilling over wooden floors for centuries, providing pubs with a sugary scent and shoe soles with a sticky layer. Instead of the young and old mix of our Exeter local, here we are surrounded exclusively by grown-ups with tanned skin – most of them by lamps or creams though some might have consolidated their shade in Mallorca or Cancun. They smile at us amicably, seizing the opportunity to inspect our chalk-whitened skins and our dirt-covered clothes in sharp contrast with their pastel blouses and shirts. Most likely they will never see us again, nor us them. How many people are there in this world who we will never meet, leading their lives in towns and cities which we will never hear about

Dinner is finished, we are back in the car, the game is restarted: who will be the first one to fall asleep from exhaustion and the lull of the pint?

Searching for Tranquillity

CHERRY BEDFORD

Life comes at me in waves; sometimes there are long peaceful lulls, calm interludes with a sense of continuity and stillness. Other times the swell picks up and I'm thrown about in the water, peaks and troughs and spray and drama. Today the sea reflects reality, my reality at least, and the waves, when I drop over the headland, are crashing in fierce, majestic beauty, unexpected under the tranquil, blue sky.

I'm here at Hartland Quay on the north coast of Devon to climb, but really I'm here to escape from my stormy, turbulent week. My friends arrive and their excited chatter picks me up, floating my battered soul. We carry our massive, padded bouldering mats down over the edge of the cliffs to the beach below. The tourists and walkers look on bemused as our over-burdened mule train goes past. Our destination is a small section of overhanging rock, maybe 5 metres high and 12 metres long. On a coastline liberally littered with bits of rock, this particular section holds some of the best bouldering in the South West. Bouldering is climbing protected only by padded mats; it's not normally very high but, as a result, each move is desperately hard. It follows, therefore, that gravity and friction are the two forces with which a climber has a very close relationship. This warm afternoon the rock feels frictionless under my sweaty fingertips.

I squeeze my feet into tight climbing shoes that help my toes feel, and stick to, the smallest fossilised ripples in the rock. Dusting white, absorbent chalk onto my hands, I start to warm up, try to remember the feel of movement in a vertical plane, try to remember that elusive sense of calm that climbing has brought me through the years. When my muscles and tendons feel suitably ready for the challenge I head over to the boulder problem I want to try. Arguably the crux, the hardest move, is the first one, pulling your weight off your bum and onto precisely placed hands and feet. I try. I fail. I know that getting frustrated will get me nowhere, but a frustrating week is battering at my consciousness and I'm struggling to keep my mind on the task at hand. Climbing in this form, with each move at the limit of one's physical ability, requires the concerted effort of nearly all the muscles in the body (even the facial muscles come into play, contorting the climber's face into a grimace of sheer will and effort). I so desperately want the high that success brings that I forget that I am here for the process, for the trying and the failing, for the tiny changes in body position that unlock a move, for the wild beauty of the coastline and for the companionship of my friends.

Perhaps my friend notices my emotional state or

perhaps the June heat is getting to him, too; he suggests a swim and Mother Nature provides the perfect swimming pool. Tucked away in the rocks and filled twice a day by the high tide, there's an oversized rock pool, mirror flat, only occasionally splashed by a rogue wave from the receding tide below. The cool, clear water soothes my hot skin and placates my mind. There's something magical about being immersed in water – maybe it speaks to our foetal selves or further back still to our evolutionary past. It could just be that the sensation overwhelms our senses with the homogeneity of water against skin. The chemist, writer and keen mountaineer Primo Levi said, '...the sea's only gifts are harsh blows and, occasionally, the chance to feel strong...' Did he never experience this? The chance to feel healed by the sea?

I return to the piece of rock, jubilant and invigorated, ready in mind and body for the challenge it presents. The sun trips slowly westward, on and down, as more and more climbers appear. The area below the rockface is now padded with a kaleidoscope of multicoloured mats, constantly changing as each climber attempts to perfect the layout of mats over the uneven rocks. On the rock itself fingers grip, muscles bulge and sinews tighten. A multinational spray of words pushes each climber up and on, to the very limit of their strength. '*Venga!*', '*Allez!*', 'Come on!' More often than not, gravity claims the victory and the climber drops into a sea of supporting arms but occasionally one fights back and claims a win over that omnipotent force. I am one of the victors, bringing my composed mind to focus on the subtleties of body position, force and momentum. My friends celebrate my achievement with genuine pleasure (as I do theirs) and we bump fists, the international symbol of pride in the effort and attainment of others.

The sea, despite its gifts, is a strict taskmaster and so we keep a weather eye on the tide that edges towards us to cut off our path out. We gather our things and, once again loaded high, walk away from something that means more to all of us than just a piece of rock. It's a place of belonging, of fellowship, of achievement. It's a calm lull between the waves of everyday life.

Black A Tor Copse

ABBY CRAWFORD

During my childhood, there was always an annual tradition where my auntie, uncle and cousins from Surrey would come down and we would all go walking on Dartmoor, often during the Christmas holidays. Me, Emma, James and Amy would bundle into the back of their sleek black jeep, wrapped up in woolly scarves and raincoats. One particular adventure took us to the moor at night. The sky stretched endlessly above, completely clear and unclouded by pollution. I perched in the open car boot, staring up at the star-studded infinite, trying to catch a glimpse of a shooting star. I don't recall now what I wanted to wish for back then. That night Uncle Michael, with his booming voice, recounted to me the legend of the Beast of Bodmin, an elusive phantom panther that haunts the moor. Although the legend originated in Cornwall, it still ignited my imagination and I believed a similar creature could perhaps inhabit Dartmoor. Within the depths of my being, a certain awareness stirred, an instinctual apprehension that whispered of a presence lurking in the shadows, an elusive creature, prowling the edges of my consciousness. Amongst my cousins, I always seemed to be the most afraid.

In those days, we also embarked on expeditions to search for empty bullet casings near the army firing range. Golden glitters of treasure amongst bracken and gorse. We polished them until their brass gleamed. Once we returned to my grandmother's farmhouse, we'd line them up neatly on the table with a certain sense of satisfaction. Other remnants also stand out in my memory: discarded jaw bones that looked almost prehistoric, racks of sheep ribs, with flesh still clinging off the bone. It always left me with a sense of unease, a landscape which was so unknowably vast and full of reminders of mortality. My cousins would grow older and move away and the trips would become less frequent. Years later, we would return to scatter Grandmother's ashes at the top of Belstone Tor. Since moving to the city, I have often revisited Dartmoor, of course, but always sticking to well-trodden paths or accompanied by friends, never fully venturing out to thoroughly explore.

Recently I decide to return. My friend Daniel proposes we go on a walk, so we hop on the recently re-established train from Exeter St David's to Okehampton. Equipped with the orange walking map and the OS map on his phone, he seems to be a lot more capable than me, even though I'm the one who has grown up in the area. He explains he has only recently started walking in the UK, but wants to encourage people to have the confidence to veer off the usual paths, to discover hidden gems of beauty. We both agree that convenience and comfort have diminished the sense of wonder in the world.

During our 12-mile walk, I slip and my leg falls into a rabbit hole. Daniel lifts me up with calloused hands, rough like stone. We encounter fellow hikers ill-prepared for the journey, who can't get across the river, as well as holiday-makers revelling in the area's splendour.

'You're so lucky to have this on your doorstep!' one woman exclaims.

I laboriously climb up slopes that feel almost vertical, my breath ragged. Pausing for a rest atop Yes Tor, my attention is drawn to a man meticulously capturing a selfie, his focus solely on the act of documenting. This triggers a reflection in me. How can we transcend the need for photos or written accounts to validate our experiences? To become living testaments to the land and breathe life between the crevices of rock? I am reminded of reading about how various tribes and indigenous peoples, through deep connection with the landscape, often wove myths and legends into the fabric of the terrain. By associating specific geographic features with mythological events or characters, they created a living tapestry that weaved their cultural heritage with the physical landscape. When the colonisers came, they didn't just ravage the land, but dismantled their intricate tapestry of myth and history.

After a while of walking and seeing nothing but clitter, scattered shrubs and gorse, we reach Black A Tor Copse. It lies left of the River Okement on a slope, a kind of verdant cleave in the landscape where ancient oak trees grow procumbent and warm boulders slumber with moss. There feels something magical about it, stumbling across an untouched grove. Although not as extensively written about as somewhere like Wistman's Wood, when I research later, I come across an account by a woman called Lady Bray who once visited. She had expressed her musings about the presence of druids inhabiting the woods and gathering mistletoe from the dwarf oaks. I find it funny that I harbour similar thoughts and our shared viewpoints intertwine across time.

Although I came away wanting to write about Dartmoor with my own imaginative visions and memories of wild, untameable heathland, the truth is that the ungulates tame the land, and it is more ordered than appears. The growth of oak trees is often stunted by the sheep eating the acorns, but in the copse, boulders offer protection and stop the animals grazing. For some reason as we walk, Daniel likes to shout obscenities at every sheep we come across in his midlands accent.

'Look at them. They just have nothing behind the eyes.'

I do wonder if they are judging me for my inferior

mastication ability, as I eat a tough bit of sourdough.

We sit on the rocks a while, and do nothing in particular. It is unusual to be held like this in the palm of silence, far from the indecency of cars. We briefly discuss Heidegger and being aware of being. I do up my shoelaces which have come loose. The copse used to be much more expansive. Apparently a man called William Chastie once killed a white stag here. I imagine the ghostly form leaping through the trees, his blood being absorbed into the growan soil. If the trees could talk, I wonder what they would say. Their branches seem to twist round themselves, like forgotten mythologies. When we return to civilisation, walking the bridge that crosses the motorway, I feel my whole self has been scrubbed clean. My sockets sing with skylarks. Contemplating the journey of an acorn, I marvel at how it surpasses its own limitations, evolving into its destined form, a manifestation far greater than its initial self, held tightly within its shell. I reflect on myself, once small and shy, having found more fertile soil and boulders that have offered protection. Now, I come to realise the significance of remembering my origins and embracing my own humble beginnings, as a young girl raised in Okehampton. To share personal stories and stitch myself into the landscape I grew up in, and promote a deeper ecology with the land. I have to draw up from the roots that have always been with me, right where I have always stood.

WYL MENMUIR

GUEST WRITER, JULY 2022

Wyl Menmuir is an award-winning author based in Cornwall. His 2016 debut novel, *The Many* was longlisted for the Man Booker Prize and was an *Observer* Best Fiction of the year pick. His second novel *Fox Fires* was published in 2021 and his short fiction has been published by Nightjar Press, Kneehigh Theatre and National Trust Books, and appeared in *Best British Short Stories*. A former journalist, Wyl has written for Radio 4's *Open Book*, *The Guardian* and *The Observer*, and the journal *Elementum*. He is co-creator of the Cornish Writing Centre, The Writers' Block, and lectures in creative writing at Falmouth University. Born in Stockport in 1979, Wyl now lives on Cornwall's north coast with his wife and two children. When he is not writing or teaching writing, Wyl enjoys messing around in boats.

Wyl's first full-length non-fiction book, *The Draw of the Sea*, won the Roger Deakin Award from the Society of Authors. Its Exeter launch took place at Quay Words.

The Draw of the Sea
Wave Rider

WILL MENMUIR

I have watched the surfers here ever since we arrived. I have watched them from the shoreline as the sun dipped into the sea behind small, perfectly formed peelers and from up on the cliffs on winter days when the waves were like steam trains at full tilt, the white smoke of their chimneys whipping back as they powered towards the land, the riders on them all but invisible aside from the lines they carved on the wave face.

I have spent hours watching shortboarders trammelling down the line, all speed and power, exploding off the lip or switching back at the peak, throwing up a ring of spray against which they were momentarily silhouetted, and bodyboarders slotting into low, green, barrelling waves. And in the summer, I've watched hordes of beginners with their unplanned yelps of delight as they found their feet on a wave for the first time, a wave that I imagined followed them home and saw them through some dark hour in the office in the winter months.

One Saturday this summer, while I was drying on

the sand after an hour's plunge in the foam, I watched a friend on his longboard. The waves were perhaps 4 or 5 feet, the breeze blowing gently offshore and all the day's colours were bleached out by the high sun. It was the sort of day that deserved its own soundtrack; something soulful with a clean, jangling guitar line, a Hammond organ, a harmonica and drums driving the whole thing.

Despite a crowded line-up, it was easy enough to pick him out: he has a distinct silhouette. Even sitting on his board, he was tall, a head above most of the other surfers bobbing on their boards out beyond the breaking waves, which arrive in lines perpendicular to the shore, peeling off to the right as they approached the beach. He paddled into one and, in the glare, I lost him for a moment. When I saw him next, he was on his feet and had picked up speed. From where I was sitting, he appeared to float on the wave. On land, he is all skinniness and angles, but on the water, he is pure grace. He held his shoulders low and his hands loose by his side as he shifted his balance now forward now back, as he worked with the wave, as it broke more quickly, as it slowed, as it surged forward, deep blue crested with white. As I watched, he adjusted his trim and cross-stepped to the front of the board, his hands raised to just below chest level, as though he was performing a well-rehearsed dance step. He balanced, toes on the board's nose, first one foot, then two, knees slightly bent, chest back, perfectly balanced, the board locked into the wave, and I could almost hear the soundtrack swell above the hush of the breakers.

Off the water, he was going through a hard time, this particular surfer. His father, who lives a few hours' drive away, was seriously ill and he was spending most of his time, when he was not working or looking after his children, on the A30, driving up and back, up and back, shuttling between fatherhood and childhood, balancing the challenging demands of both, and the challenges of work too. For these few seconds, though, on the wave, he appeared to be weightless, a featherlight figure who had perfected the trick of walking on water. The whole event, though it lasted just seconds, seemed to bend time slightly, and it appeared to me rendered in slight slow motion. Like the surfer who slips into the green room of a barrelling wave and emerges, as though spat out by the spray created in the hollow tube, what he was doing – hanging ten – represents, in surfing terms, a pinnacle moment, an expression of years of hard-earned skill and practice, of balance, timing, wave reading and wave riding.

It's easy to think of surfing in terms of the pinnacle moments achieved by these who have dedicated a good part of their lives to the waves. The initiated often talk about these moments in semi-religious terms. It's hard to describe the ineffable.

It is all but guaranteed that if the surf is up here, whatever time of year, there will already be riders on the wave before you get there, no matter how early. This is Badlands – deep surfing country.

Serious surf is reserved for early risers and for the most committed who sleep on thin mattresses amid their boards in their vans within earshot of the waves. It is reserved for those who can calculate the length of the fetch, the wave period and height, those who can accurately predict where the best waves will be found. In his surf memoir, *Barbarian Days*, William Finnegan points out that there is no agreed standard measure for wave height among the surfing community. Novice surfers, he writes, tend to vastly overestimate the height of the wave, while veterans downplay it. Finnegan cites the wife of a big wave surfer who claimed she could accurately calculate the height of a wave in refrigerators, which seems to me as good a measure as any.

The serious surfers attempt to predict the effects of a hurricane on the American eastern seaboard or a depression in the mid-Atlantic on a reef or a beach break several hundred miles east, the way a particular wave is likely to react to a particular profile of beach. They are the most genned-up of amateur meteorologists. When it is *on*, messages are exchanged on WhatsApp and locations agreed, and those in the know converge, having concluded that this particular place at this particular time might offer the best of the day's waves.

When a builder we employed shortly after we moved here disappeared a week into the job, we assumed another urgent job had come up or perhaps a family emergency. It transpired there was a forecast that the wave at Thurso, on Scotland's north coast, was about to go off and he had dropped everything for it. He had jumped in his van and headed north for the 820-mile drive. If the prediction was correct, the wave at the out-of-the-way reef break would be worth it. The wave at Thurso East is generally known to be one of the finest right-handers in Europe, a large barrelling wave that – aside from the frigid conditions – would not be out of place on the Hawaiian coast. It is not as though there are no ridable waves on our doorstep here; it is more that the temptation is undeniable for some surfers. It is not unusual for a builder, a plumber, an electrician, a decorator or postman here to travel with a board and wetsuit in the van, just in case. When the surf is good, it is surprising how no one seems to have that much urgent work to do (well, if you are a surfer, really not that surprising at all). It's one of the prices and privileges of living here, an unwritten addendum to pretty much any contract on the north coast.

If the surf is good, I'll be late.

If it's really good, I'll see you once the swell has passed.

As the Cornish are fond of saying, *I'll be with you dreckly*.

Extract from *The Draw of the Sea*,
Wyl Menmuir, Aurum Press, 2022,
reprinted with permission.

KIM SHERWOOD

GUEST WRITER, MAY 2023

Kim Sherwood is an author and creative writing lecturer. Born in Camden in 1989, she has taught at the University of Sussex, UWE, and in schools, libraries and prisons, and now lectures at the University of Edinburgh, where she lives in the city. Her first novel, *Testament*, published in 2018, won the Bath Novel Award and the *Harper's Bazaar* Big Book of the Year, was shortlisted for the Author's Club Best First Novel Award and was longlisted for the Desmond Elliott Prize. In 2019, Kim was shortlisted for the *Sunday Times* Young Writer of the Year Award. Kim is currently writing a trilogy of *Double O* novels for the Ian Fleming Estate, expanding the James Bond universe with new heroes for the twenty-first century. The first title, *Double or Nothing*, was published by HarperCollins in the UK and William Morrow will publish it in the US in 2023. Kim Sherwood came to Exeter Custom House for a reading and Q&A about her latest novel, *A Wild & True Relation*. Combining smuggling and literary history, the novel is a perfect fit for the Exeter Custom House venue. The event opened the Quayside's first Heritage Festival.

A Wild & True Relation
March Comes in Like a Lion

KIM SHERWOOD

Tom's arms folded around her, and Molly knew she was safe. Most of the crew couldn't swim, but Tom insisted Molly learn. The *Escape* was anchored in the Channel. Kingston and Nathan looked on, tension in them, Molly sensed, afraid of the water, or afraid of Tom, who'd demanded she swim, though she cried at the thought of such cold depths. Tom dived off the back of the ship. Benedict threw out the lifeline, a coil that cut the sky, quickly drawn taut by the pull of the tide. Tom took hold of it, and called for Molly to jump. Her heart slammed against her ribs, but Tom was looking at her with such belief, she didn't want that look to fade. So she hurled herself into the air, hitting water, which threatened to yank her bones right out – but there were Tom's arms, grabbing her; there was Tom's hand, guiding her own to the lifeline; there was the calm steadiness of Tom treading water, and so Molly rested in the shelter of his chest and followed his movements. Pride warmed her as Benedict whooped from the deck, and, in her ear, Tom whispered, 'That's my boy. That's my boy.'

The *Escape* slipped through the dawn haze, running down wind, fore-and-aft sails taut. The striped wall of red rock and green roots between Scabbacombe Head and Outer Froward Point was still; no candlelight winked from the fishermen's cottages or flashed from the rocks, no warnings to the free-traders that Revenue were about; no lures for ships in a storm, inviting them onto the rock.

Tom stood at the bow with his head back a little, listening to the ship's song. Murmuring wind, the slosh of breaking waves; no whistle from loose caulking or groan from rotting timbers. Just Hellard, running his mouth to Nathan. Prell, Kingston and van Meijer up the riggings. Pascale at the whipstaff, a Frenchman who had sailed for the Sun King before free-trading from the cold Norfolk coast, across the marshes of Kent, to the golden sands of Devon. Laskey the Pole, and One-Eyed Jarvis, old hands both; Shaun, once a press-ganged gunner for King William; and, of course, Benedict. Most free-traders changed crews as often as they patched their sails, but Tom's crew was fixed. They were his men. Though, listening to Hellard peddling blindmares, a man might come under the illusion that the *Escape* had a different master.

Tom leant over the gunwale, let the spray drown out Hellard. The sea's cold fingers got inside his shirt. He stroked the wet timber – the tar flaking from his nights spent picking at it. Below, the hold was filled with oilskin bundles, citrus tea clouding the usual stench of unwashed men, reminding Tom of Spanish lemon trees in the rain. He took a breath, dragging the sea to the depths of his body, and then ducked beneath the throat halyard and swung around the main mast to the whipstaff. Pascal tipped his hat and moved to the peak halyard.

'Coming about!'

'Ready!'

Tom seized the tiller as the men let out the gib until they were even-keeled. No pressure, no wind, a sudden peace, bearing away from Dartmouth. Tom watched the quay, the stacked houses and the shops, the castle over the mouth of the river. The *Escape* was larger than most smuggling vessels, a danger if a Revenue cruiser came looking, but there was strength in size: strength that meant he could, and would, turn and fight. He searched for temptation from the hilltops, for a plume over Dick English's chimneys.

The night he told Molly that English survived the fire, she had grown lost in her reflection, warped by the blade of the knife she played with. She pressed the tip into the boards.

'That's how I'd kill Dick English,' she said, and she sounded, suddenly, so much older.

Tom had wiped his face, promising her, 'If it's justice you want...' Then he hesitated, as she tilted the knife, catching something of his shade. 'If it's justice you want – we'll have it, you and I.'

But today he saw no sign of life from the home of Dick English. His eyesight dated him every month of his two and thirty years. But he still had the youth of others. Where was Benedict?

Tom called for his spotsman. Quick steps below, the clunk of the hatch opening, and then Benedict slid towards him, the *Escape* pitching into squally water.

'Give your eyes unto the Lord, my lad,' said Tom.

Benedict forced the telescope open, steadying himself against Tom's shoulder like a child learning to skate – still so like a child, though now one and twenty. Tom had given him the telescope when he first came aboard, fresh from Kingsbridge Grammar School. His eyes were as good at deciphering close-set scripture as they proved to be spotting hidden rocks and eddies. The crew said he carried a constant look of shock with him now, like a virgin after his first good niggle, eyes swollen enough to take in all the coast's secrets.

'Nought following,' said Benedict. He turned to line up his transit, Dancing Beggars rocks with the spire at Stoke Fleming. 'Bearing sou' sou'west.'

Tom looked down the line of Benedict's arm, following the boy's pointing finger with the tiller.

'Sheet in!'

The sail slapped to starboard, and the *Escape*

tacked through Start Bay, Benedict muttering to himself – 'Matthew's Point to Strete Church, Limpet Rocks to Tinsey Head, Start Point to Black Stone' – the great jut of land rearing over them, and then round to Ravens Cove, Sleaden Rocks, Two Stones, and Tom called, 'Heave to!' The sails faced each other, the jet of wind between them a sigh of relief, and the *Escape* drifted to a stop.

Benedict realised he was still holding on to Tom's shoulder, and looked up at the captain with a shy smile.

Tom winked at him.

Tom's father had told him, *When in danger, run to sea.* He meant it plainly, of course: that it's better to turn from the coast and head back out to sea if you don't know the rocks, even if there's a storm set to drown you. The most dangerous part of the run was landing, and if it weren't for Benedict they'd have run aground more than once. A spotsman needed local lore, but, more than that, a gift for memory, a gift for sight.

When Tom had first set out to sea, his mother begged him, You're in no danger, there's no need to run. The danger awaits you out there. He'd told her, I know. I'm looking for it. And she wept.

Extract from *A Wild & True Relation*, Kim Sherwood, Virago Press, 2023, reprinted with permission.

DAVINA QUINLIVAN

WRITER-IN-RESIDENCE, SPRING 2023

Davina Quinlivan is a Lecturer in the Department of
English and Creative Writing at The University of
Exeter. Her memoir, *Shalimar: A Story of Place and
Migration*, was published by Little Toller Books (2022)
and her creative non-fiction essays and short stories
have appeared in *The Willowherb Review*, *Litro*, *Arty*, *The
Clearing*, *Caught by the River*, and in collaboration with
The Countryside Alliance and The Museum of
English Rural Life. Her work has featured as part of
programmed, public events of The Wallace
Collection, The Wellcome Trust, The Urban Tree
Festival and The Serpentine Gallery. For several years,
she has run the popular seminar series *F: For Flânerie* at
The Freud Museum, and is part of the founding
teaching ensemble at The New School of the
Anthropocene, alongside Marina Warner and Robert
Macfarlane. *Shalimar* was selected by Spiracle
Audiobooks as one of stories which would launch
their new audiobook platform in 2022. Prior to
moving to Exeter, she taught for twelve years as a
Senior Lecturer at The School of Art, Kingston
University. She is currently working on a follow-up to
Shalimar entitled *Waterlines*, on rivers and migration,

trauma and healing, and a novel set between Cornwall and the Black Sea.

In March and April 2023 Davina was chosen for a shared writer residency both at Quay Words and at the Devon & Exeter Institution for a season focused on the theme of 'Threads', diving into Exeter's rich textile history and present-day connections.

The Wool-Dyer's Hands

DAVINA QUINLIVAN

Her finger points out a shape in the sky,
Caiseoipé, then *an Leon* and *an Scairp*,
burn bright over Dartmoor.

Enchantment in her infant's eyes,
mother and child swaddled in their patchwork
breath.

Her dreams shiver and fold into each other's night,
an obsidian geology: Haldon Hill, Brampford Speke,
a half-forgotten chapel on the Culm.

Thought is buried in time,
soil-scattered rhyme, beneath the where or how
of all things lost.

Lyme's fossils cannot compare to
the relic of her mother's hands,
their gentle voyage around a fallen russet.

Interpreter of skies,
plucking at the pegs on her washing line.
Three days' rain will empty any sky.

Clutch of ice at a window,
dawn suspended between her palms.
She boils water drawn from the River Exe.
Liquid mirror, it had carried the flight of three geese
and a raven over Fore Street,
curved shadow line of two swans near St Thomas.

All the spilt, tiny ruins
of pebbles, siltstone, Devon clay,
hay fallen from a cart near Rewe.

Then once more through the passage of the ships in
the Quay
and the ancient hymn of the cattle market.
A murmuration of starlings dissolved by a single flame.

Dim reflection in the eye of a barn owl,
burial ground for three field mice in the river reeds.
Clouds make a memory of the air.

A falling dust beckons a strange forest
which once was the kitchen table.
Like this, she is able to alter the weather of her house.

Quiet, concentrated assembly of her tools,
wooden spoon and tongs, a measurement of iron,
particles of copper, gorse flowers, undyed skein.

Familiar spell, sinuous smell of oak bark, moss and
alum,
their flight between her fingers
before they meet the hidden language of the river and
the shepherd's fold.

In the city, her city, the men use the dyeing frames up
on Exe Island,
rackfields in the summer, matted cloth on tenterhooks.
Coins for the Crown, s*traites* for the County.*

But she has made a rack of the orchards and her trees
are her frames.
Feral fibred object,
ghost of her mother's hands.

* In 1513, a law was passed by King Henry VIII permitting
Devon wool-makers to produce *straites*, a type of light-weight,
white woollen trouser.

Threads

A 'living' poem produced by members of the local community in Exeter City, created as part of a workshop with Writer-in-Residence Davina Quinlivan.

A small, neat ball of soft, pure wool, or
remains of clothing.
The shepherd nurtured and sheared the sheep.
The flock mooch and munch contentedly
in the Exe Valley orchards,
far away from their ancestral home in Shropshire.

Rich in colour, soft and snug,
a gift from Chinese neighbours newly come,
reflects an unexpected love.

Red, it's my colour,
the cuffs rippling in the wind,
Hung lazily off an arm.

You don't know where I'm from,
you don't see the labour,
you see Skye, deep time,
distant, convenient distractions.
Hand-made and sold by women in rural India.
The green scarf – practical, beautiful, but humble.
Protects me, as it did then. It offers
priceless shelter from a sometimes harsh world.

A square of muslin, one of many, is textured and dense.
When used, it expands to become fine and smooth.
Later, my son will ask me to tie it around his small shoulders
as a Superhero cloak.
He wears it throughout the first year of school,
which coincides with the end of his parents' relationship.
His eyes, my eyes – back and forth.

Red, stripy headscarf protects age ten,
red tartan wraps my belly seven years on,
the place that warms three boys, then cushions mum,
clutching her handkerchief as she gasps.

Her remembered home I took with me,
The double-sided shawl of crimson irony
Like my friend who gave it me, she sang:
'Dance with the colour, swim with the sea,' trust the
space between my yarn, endlessly.

ROGER ROBINSON
and JOHNY PITTS

GUEST WRITER AND PHOTOGRAPHER, FEBRUARY 2023

Roger Robinson is the winner of the 2019 T.S. Eliot Prize and the 2020 RSL Ondaatje Prize. He was chosen by Decibel as one of fifty writers who have influenced the Black British writing canon. His latest collection, *A Portable Paradise*, was a *New Statesman* book of the year. He is an alumnus of The Complete Works and was shortlisted for the OCM Bocas Poetry Prize, The Oxford Brookes Poetry Prize and the 2020 Derek Walcott Prize for Poetry, as well as being commended by the Forward Poetry Prize. He is the lead vocalist and lyricist for King Midas Sound and has also recorded solo albums with Jahtari Records. Roger was elected a Fellow of the Royal Society of Literature in 2020.

Johny Pitts is a writer, photographer and broadcaster known for his work in exploring African–European identities. He is the curator of the European Network Against Racism (ENAR) award-winning afropean.com, and the author of *Afropean: Notes from Black Europe*.

In recognition of his work, he has received the Jhalak Prize, the Bread and Roses Award for Radical Publishing, the Leipzig Book Award for European Understanding and the European Essay Prize. The recipient of the inaugural Ampersand/Photoworks Fellowship, his photography has been exhibited at Foam (Amsterdam), E-Werk (Freiburg) and the Museum of Contemporary Photography (Chicago).

Roger and Johny joined forces to produce *Home Is Not a Place*. Featuring photographs, poetry and essays, it reflects on the complexity, strength and resilience of Black Britain. The two authors explore the question 'What is it like to be black in Britain today, particularly if you live outside the urban, metropolitan centres?'

The event at Quay Words was co-produced by Speaking Volumes, Sprung Sultan and Coastal Carolina University.

Home Is Not a Place
The Quality of Light

ROGER ROBINSON

A Saint Lucian and a Nigerian are talking
about the quality of light, in art and writing.
Whether you describe the specific
light of where you're from or the certain light
of where you live. Whether you can describe
the quality of light and/or occupy that light
at the same time. Perhaps it has something
to do with skin, whether it remembers the sun's
slanted rays as a bronze burnish or a rose blotch.
Or maybe you prefer the marine light
from the salted roar of waves or the bluegreen
light of a pond's still algae, what is lived
and what is visited, whether the frosted light
of winter evens your skin to porcelain
or dries it to ash. Maybe it's about who
you're writing for and what you're reading,
where you've lived and where you've been
and what light does to the skin you're in.

From *Home Is Not a Place*,
Roger Robinson and Johny Pitts,
Harper Collins, 2022, reprinted with permission

Photograph by Johny Pitts from *Home Is Not a Place*, Roger
Robinson and Johny Pitts, Harper Collins, 2022,
reprinted with permission.

ANTHONY JOSEPH

GUEST WRITER, NOVEMBER 2022

Anthony Joseph is an award-winning Trinidad-born poet, novelist, academic and musician. He is the author of five poetry collections and three novels. His 2018 novel, *Kitch: A Fictional Biography of a Calypso Icon*, was shortlisted for the Republic of Consciousness Prize and the Royal Society of Literature's Encore Award, and longlisted for the OCM Bocas Prize for Caribbean Literature. His most recent publication is the experimental novel *The Frequency of Magic*. In 2019 he was awarded a Jerwood Compton Poetry Fellowship. As a musician he has released eight critically acclaimed albums and in 2020 received a Paul Hamlyn Foundation Composer's Award.

With his poetry collection *Sonnets for Albert*, presented at Quay Words, Anthony Joseph returns to the autobiographical material explored in his earlier collection *Bird Head Son*. In this follow-up he weighs the impact of being the son of an absent, or mostly absent, father.

Bird Head of Second Avenue

ANTHONY JOSEPH

On Second Avenue there was Bobby Cole, the soul
man,
dark-boned and strolling smooth in his high Clarks
boots.
Passing the school there was Sugar Bain and Half Eye
Mong,
Red Man the stevedore, Jimmy the thief, Saga Boy
the pimp.
These were my father's friends in Mt Lambert,
the ones who called him 'Bird Head' because his
head,
they said, was too small for his body. As young men
they fished
in ravines and picked fruit still warm from the vine.
My aunt Ursula tells me my father had to leave Mt
Lambert
after his stepfather drew a shotgun against him. (The
same gun
was drawn against me one night, and just the sight
of the barrel was terror enough.) Those men in Mt
Lambert
knew me before my name. All through my youth
along those avenues,

they smoked slow cigarettes and called me, 'Bird
Head Son.'

From *Sonnets for Albert*, Anthony Joseph,
Bloomsbury Poetry, 2022,
reprinted with permission.

FIONA BENSON
and KAT LYONS

GUEST WRITERS, THE HEALTH & RESILIENCE PROJECT, AUTUMN 2022

In the first in our series of events linked to The Health & Resilience Project, we welcomed poets Fiona Benson and Kat Lyons to Exeter Custom House where they explored the presentation of bodies, change, and resilience in poetry.

Fiona Benson was educated at Trinity College, Oxford and then St Andrews University, where she completed the MLitt and a PhD in Early Modern Drama. Her pamphlet was 'Faber New Poets 1' in the Faber New Poets series, and her full-length collection *Bright Travellers* (Cape, 2014) received the Seamus Heaney Prize for a first collection and the Geoffrey Faber Memorial Prize. Her second book, *Vertigo & Ghost* (Cape, 2019), won the Roehampton Poetry Prize and the Forward Poetry Prize. Her third collection is *Ephemeron* (2022). She lives in Mid Devon with her husband and their two daughters.

Kat Lyons (they/them) is a queer Bristol-based writer, performer, workshop facilitator and creative producer whose work is grounded in everyday politics and a love of storytelling. They are the current Bristol

City Poet (2022–2024) and were nominated for the Jerwood Poetry in Performance Award 2022. Kat's debut collection *Love Beneath the Nails* was published in February 2022 by Verve Poetry Press. They perform widely at poetry nights, festivals and events throughout the UK and are currently touring their first solo show, *Dry Season*, which explores menopause, age and gender.

Fly

FIONA BENSON

Spring broke out but my soul did not.
It kept to sleet and inwards fog.
Forget-me-nots around the path,
a speckled thrush; I spoke rarely
and had a sour mouth. I couldn't make love.
My husband lay beside me in the dark.
I listened till he slept. I picked out
all the bad parts of my day like sore jewels
and polished them till they hurt.
I wanted to take myself off like a misshapen jumper,
a badly fitting frock. I wanted
to peel it off and burn it in the garden
with the rubbish, pushing it deep
into the fire with a fork. And what sliver
of my stripped and pelted soul there still remained,
I'd have it gone, smoked out, shunned,
fled not into the Milky Way,
that shining path of souls, but the in-between,
the nothing. But this overshoots the mark,
this gnashing sorrow, so Wagnerian;
it was more a vague, grey element I moved in
that kept me remote and slow,
like a bound and stifled fly, half-paralysed,

drugged dumb, its soft and intermittent buzz,
its torpid struggle in the spider's sick cocoon.
What now if I call on the sublime?
What bright angels of the pharmakon
will come now if I call, and rip
this sticky gauze and tear me out?

From *Vertigo & Ghost*,
Fiona Benson, Cape Poetry, 2019,
reprinted with permission of the author.

vanishing point

KAT LYONS

remember the bugs? their bodies
smashed against our screens
the bloody smears the mess
they left

it's been a while
sometimes we look back
squint through arcs of viscera tonight
the roads are wet the air smells clean

we speed forward wipe aside
leaves weather minor inconveniences
guided by artificial eyes
follow our own reflected light to where

parallel lines converge tarmac hits
the horizon collides
with the star-crazed curve
of a sky as hard and clear as tempered glass

From *Love Beneath the Nails*,
Kat Lyons, Verve Poetry Press, 2022,
reprinted with permission.

HARULA LADD

WORKSHOP LEADER, THE HEALTH
& RESILIENCE PROJECT, AUTUMN 2022

A collaboration between Quay Words and the Wellcome Centre
for Cultures and Environments of Health,
supported by Exeter UNESCO City of Literature.

Harula is a slam-winning poet, performer and creative facilitator, with over fifteen years' experience in leading creative writing workshops. Performance highlights have included gigs with Spork!/Milk in Bristol and Hot Poets/Tongue Fu at London's Southbank Centre. Her poem 'Skin' was nominated for the Pushcart Prize in 2021.

Harula is passionate about the role of the arts and creativity in cultivating individual and collective wellbeing. She has been poet-in-residence at two conferences with the Social Prescribing Network, and also wrote poems for staff and patients at Torbay NHS Trust as part of their Reflection Day, acknowledging the impact of the pandemic on wellbeing across the organisation.

Most recently, she has facilitated sessions at Ladies Lounge and Shekinah Grow, as part of Literature Works' Community Writing Project. She also continues to co-host a monthly open (no)mic event, *Word Stir!*, at Totnes Community Bookshop.

For Quay Words, Harula facilitated a writing workshop as part of The Health & Resilience Project with Resilient Women, a community group in Exeter focused on support for women referred through the criminal justice system.

Skin

HARULA LADD

is hard to put back on at a moment's notice,
when someone knocks on your door to offer
a piece of their mother's Christmas cake.

You wipe wetness from your cheeks, demand your skin
quickly swallow you in again and keep the hand
where the skin is cracked behind your back.

Reach out with the other to receive
perfect Christmas cake, complete
with miniature marzipan holly.

You make eye contact with this new mother,
pushed to the edge of her own skin
until she's shining. She's beautiful.

***

The skin you live in is tight, thin,
bulging with broken that just wants

to breathe. At night you pin your skin
to the edges of your room, to the curtains,

hook it over the door handle, trap a corner
under the weight of a table leg so at least you can be free

while you sleep. When you wake, skin
won't shrink to fit. You wonder if you should give up

your free feeling dreams where skin is so big you can
swim in it,
inside it, exploring it from underneath like swimming
underwater

looking up at the surface not wanting to break it yet.
It's quiet and fascinating down here.

People can't knock on the surface of the sea.
They'd have to wade in and get wet to reach you,

so swim
swim
swim

First published by iambapoet.com.

An 'I Wish...' Poem

RESILIENT WOMEN

Knowing what I know now,
to learn from my mistakes
and not repeat them.
I wish I could see into the future,
and act accordingly!
I wish our country was led
by people with integrity.
I wish speed.

I wish for the pace of the world to slow down.
I wish I had more hours in the day.
I wish I was as strong and energetic
as I used to be!
I wish they wouldn't play
Christmas music so early.
I wish quiet.

I wish for good health.
I wish my children
the very best life possible,
for my children and grandchildren
to have good health.

I wish for my loved ones
to have safe journeys.
I wish to always find
purpose and beauty in the world.

I wish to live life to the fullest
with an array of experiences,
for health and happiness
for the remainder of my life.
I wish to be
who I really am.

CATHY RENTZENBRINK

MASTERCLASS TUTOR, GUEST WRITER, OCTOBER 2022

Cathy Rentzenbrink is an author and acclaimed memoirist whose books include *The Last Act of Love* and *Dear Reader*. In 2021 she published her first novel *Everyone Is Still Alive*. Her book about how to write a memoir is called *Write It All Down: How to Put Your Life on the Page* (Pan Macmillan, 2023). Cathy speaks and writes regularly on life, death, love and literature, hosts the *Bookseller* podcast, writes a column for *Prospect* and reviews books for *The Times*.

She led an intensive day-long creative writing course for Quay Words, focusing on memoir and writing from life. Cathy appeared with publisher Francesca Main. We reproduce here an extract from Cathy's moving memoir *The Last Act of Love: The Story of My Brother and His Sister*.

Cathy's Masterclass at Quay Words was produced in partnership with Arvon.

The Last Act Of Love
Snaith Hall

CATHY RENTZENBRINK

It wasn't as hard as I thought in the end. Mum looked terrible when I got home, thin and haggard. She'd had her fortieth birthday while I was away, and having always looked so pretty and young, now she was drawn and old. And Dad was piling on weight. He'd always been big and strong, but was starting to look fat. Matty, of course, was the same as always.

'Hello, old chap, *bonjour, mon vieux*,' I said.

I felt I had to put on a bit of a show for everyone else. I sat next to him for a bit, holding his hand, and as usual there was nothing, not an iota of a response. I felt a huge wave of compassion for this poor creature, this shell of a person. I couldn't believe that anyone would want to live like this – though at least, I thought, he didn't know that he lived like this. This thing, this entity, bore no relation to our Matty. I looked into his vacant eyes. I no longer expected to see any evidence of his soul; rather I hoped that there was no soul there to suffer.

'Mum looks bloody awful,' I said to Dad when we

went out for a drink together. 'I don't think she can carry on.'

'We're stuck,' said Dad. 'We don't know what to do. There isn't anything else.'

'There must be,' I said. 'Let's talk to her about it.'

The next day we all took Murphy down to the riverbank and had a long talk. We couldn't talk at home because of Matty and because of all the people who looked after him popping in and out. With the distance that being in France had given me, I could see that the bungalow was like a hospital for one person with everything revolving around Matty's care. There were notice boards with drug regimens and charts showing his temperature, pulse and respiration pinned up on them, the physio room with a tilt table, wedges and oxygen tanks. The cupboard was full of Ensure, bed linen, towels, suppositories, Epilim, convenes, bags for urine. My parents' lives were not a priority. They had little privacy – they shared a bedroom with Matty – and not much identity beyond being part of Matty's care team. Perhaps at one time, when there was a prospect of improvement, this huge subjugation of the rest of the family had felt like a good and right thing. Now it seemed perverse. It felt like the three of us were sitting on Matty's funeral pyre and refusing to get off.

'I don't think this can go on, Mum,' I said as we watched Murphy swimming for sticks.

'I know it's mad,' she said. 'I know he doesn't know where he is or who we are, but what can we do? We've seen hospital wards where no one cleans a wet or soiled bed unless visitors are expected. We can't do that to Matty, whether he's aware of it or not.'

We talked to our GP about our plight, and he arranged a week's respite care in Goole hospital to give us time to formulate a plan.

We had been offered a hospital place at Scunthorpe or Goole on Matty's discharge from Leeds all that time ago, but now it was made clear that a permanent hospital bed was no longer on offer, so we visited various care homes in the area. But none of the staff seemed to understand that it was possible to have as non-existent a level of response as Matty did.

'Oh, you can leave him here without any worries,' said a breezy matron. 'Just let us know his signals, his yes and his no, and we can do exactly what you would do.'

If he had signals for yes and no we wouldn't be here, I thought, and we got out of there as fast as we could.

We found the ideal solution in our own village, a small care home called Snaith Hall run by a kind family who knew us and knew the story. We wanted to have our own carer come in each day to do his bath, so that we could be sure he wasn't overlooked if they were busy.

'It's not necessary,' said gentle Mr McEnroe in his

soft Irish accent. 'We'll care for him well. But if it helps you to do that then we have no problem with it.'

In August, five years after the accident, Matty was moved into Snaith Hall. Sue had helped with Matty's care in the bungalow and was happy to go into the Hall every day to do his bath. Mum went to visit every Sunday and sat with him for an hour or two, reading from the papers. I went with her the first time but found it too sad to see him there. Although I knew this was the best solution, although the Hall was very pleasant, although I knew Matty wasn't aware of anything, I still felt terribly guilty at the thought of him being there alone.

When I was getting ready to go again the next Sunday, Mum asked if I was sure I wanted to.

'You don't have to, you know.'

'Then I won't,' I said.

I was grateful to be spared, and I didn't go again. Now that I thought it would be better for Matty if he died, I didn't know how to be with his physical body.

One night I was serving behind the bar when a young man asked me if I was Cathy. He said he knew my brother.

'Oh,' I said, surprised I didn't know him. 'That must have been a long time ago.'

'No,' he said. 'I'm a care assistant up at the Hall. I look after him.'

I felt a bit sick. He was smiling at me, clearly just wanting to make friends, but I felt invaded.

You'll know I don't visit him then, I wanted to say, but didn't. So why would you think I'd want to chat about him over the bar?

As far as possible, I tried to put Matty out of my mind. Books helped. Booze helped. I spent the summer working in the pub, drinking hard at every opportunity. We often did lock-ins, just a few, very trusted customers at the end of the night for an extra couple of drinks. No one paid for anything; we thought of it as having people over in our own house. Mum and Dad would go to bed, and I'd stay up half the night drinking and joking. We'd turn off all the lights in the pub except the bar lights, and we'd invent drinks, setting up rounds of flaming Drambuie, seeing which spirits would go well with Guinness. I trained myself to like Campari that summer and learned how to open bottles of beer with my teeth. All I had to do was stay sober enough to lock the door and set the burglar alarm.

Britpop had arrived, and the summer unfolded to the sound of Pulp's 'Common People' playing again and again on the jukebox. My parents and I felt liberated, could take days out together without having to arrange cover for Matty, could go back to the bungalow and not be faced with his blank stare.

One sunny afternoon in late August we went to

York. We had a long lunch and then Mum went off shopping while Dad and I had a drink outside the King's Head on the riverbank. We loved this pub. It had a picture of Richard III on its sign and marks inside that showed the levels the water got to every time it flooded, which it did every couple of years or so.

There was a carnival atmosphere – men with no shirts on sitting on the bridge over the river.

'They'll start jumping in as the day goes on,' Dad said.

On the next table a group of Geordie lads who had lost all their money at the races were earning their fare home by eating live wasps for £1 a time. They'd trap them in an empty pint pot, get the pound, and then pop them into their mouths. There were plenty of takers, and once they'd raised enough money they strolled off to the train station.

In the middle of all the joviality, Dad and I were deep in talk. We both felt that even though life was much better for us since Matty had gone into the nursing home, it was really no better for him. Would he want to be in a home with old people, unable to speak, move, or express an opinion? Would he want his food pumped into his stomach, his dribble wiped, his pee collected in a bag, his poo controlled by suppositories? We both agreed that it would be better for him if he died. The Tony Bland case had alerted us to a legal path. No pillows over his head, no overdosing on the medication.

Mum came back from shopping and sat down next to us.

'We've been talking about Tony Bland,' I said.

Her face crumpled.

'I'm not ready,' she said. 'Let me get used to the nursing home first. I'm not ready to talk about anything else yet.'

We agreed we wouldn't bring it up again until she raised it.

As we gathered our stuff and left, I saw that the couple at the next table were staring at us. I realized that we probably sounded like we were planning a murder.

Extract from *The Last Act of Love*,
Cathy Rentzenbrink, Picador, 2015,
reprinted with permission.

JOHN WEDGWOOD CLARKE

GUEST WRITER, MAY 2023

John was born and raised in Cornwall. He trained as an actor at the Guildhall School of Music and Drama before going on to study literature and complete a PhD in 'Objectivist' Poetry at the University of York. He is an Associate Professor in Creative Writing at the University of Exeter. His first poetry collection *Ghost Pot* (2013) was described by Bernard O'Donoghue as a 'masterpiece that rewards continual re-reading'. Clarke's poetry often grows out of collaborations with scientists and artists, and is displayed in art galleries, museums and in the landscape. His credits as TV presenter and researcher for BBC Four include *Through the Lens of Larkin* (2017) and *Cornwall's Red River* (2021) which is based on his research project about a post-industrial river in West Cornwall. His latest collection, *Boy Thing* (2023), was launched at Quay Words.

Boy Thing

xxix

JOHN WEDGWOOD CLARKE

Earth hums my heart
beating into the shape
of the communal refuse shed.

Blowflies flash
through light blades
like fused-glass asteroids,

their deep-throated
amplified buzz in webs
strung through me.

In the bin-day bins,
Page 3 Girls call
from tea-bag cockled newspapers,

fag ashy, cradling
grapefruit whitely deflating
to sweet soil.

As if all know the look
and order of their waste,
I memorise stratigraphies

of crispy-pancake rind,
fish-finger carapace,
clumped tissue,

reconstruct moments
of disposal after reading
strange matter:

Voyager flies by Saturn's rings;
Diana's silk dress whispers
the steps of St. Paul's;

GOTCHA! explodes into
The Belgrano
lives drowning in

sticky-inked headlines,
in tits slick with baby oil,
pull-out paper flags.

From *Boy Thing*,
John Wedgwood Clarke,
Arc Publications, 2023, reprinted with permission.

CALEB PARKIN

COMMUNITY WRITING PRACTITIONER, JULY 2022

Caleb Parkin, Bristol City Poet 2020–2022, won second prize in the National Poetry Competition 2016 and the Winchester Poetry Prize 2017. His poems have been published in *The Rialto*, *The Poetry Review*, *Under the Radar*, *Poetry Wales*, *Magma*, *Butcher's Dog*, *Lighthouse* and elsewhere. Caleb tutors for the Poetry Society, the Poetry School, Cheltenham Festivals and First Story. He holds an MSc in Creative Writing for Therapeutic Purposes (CWTP). His latest collection of poetry is *wasted rainbow* (tall-lighthouse, 2021). You can discover more of Caleb's work at www.calebparkin.com.

For Quay Words he led a creative workshop for Headway Devon, a charity in Exeter dedicated to improving life after brain injury.

Why Are You Crying, Boy? (Part 2)

Section 28, 1988–2003

Nothing in the playground's sharp corners, where
dust
loiters, whirlwinds of divided Twix, frozen Penguins.

Nothing in brutalist corners, where Wispa wrappers
mutter
invitations to brittle leaves and shuffle dance among
the fag-butts.

Nothing in canteen corners where we, the
unappetising, chew greasy
pizza, suck up sickly pink milk, all eyes on the
counter's steel horizon.

Nothing lodged among the chewed gum beneath
picnic benches, drip
dripping stalactites of apathy, merging our unheard
voices in these

corners of fractured brick. Nothing sat, framing the practice rooms,
where minor chords congregate with sticky bows and covert song.

Nothing in the corners of every playing field, where we recoil
from ourselves, kicks balls and faces; until the rubbish parades

from Kit-Kat red, to cheese and onion green, and Yorkie purple
and arches away into a pale sky, a perfectly wasted rainbow.

From *wasted rainbow*, Caleb Parkin,
tall-lighthouse, 2021,
reprinted with permission.

Our Manifesto

Headway Devon

I am for a group that is inclusive
where we understand respectfully
share manners   nature
where humans are together
with the rest of the Planet
instead of destroying it   as we are

I don't want
people to feel judged   boycott judgement!
nastiness or people being unkind
any viruses that seem to be round and about

I want understanding   knowledge
to know how I can get there
writing that is clear and easy to understand and
interpret
to be treated as an equal and like I am approachable
to clear the world of Putins!

We want   company   everyone
starts where they are   gives space to others
positive outlook but allowing what's underneath
to access all art in a clear form for people's benefit

for people to be kind to each other
to speak kind and treat others kind
to treat everybody with respect and get on well
to feel I've done quite well
to learn start and has a finish

We need   to be aware of everything going on
around us
to have a fair crack at this and let others shine
a patient outlook allowing for negativity
a lot of help in our poetry group
prompts to take forward with our poetry
to learn different types of poetry

When we leave poetry   happy   uplifted
more confident   pleased that we have done
a good poem   listened to each other

Writing is a nightmare   I do not know full stop
comment   capital letter   write a letter
We do not want spelling checks

We want to write about
the world   politics, money, art, nature
how I feel about everything and everybody
about feelings, thoughts and actions
making your own coffee

ANDREW MILLER

SHORT COURSE TUTOR, HOTHOUSE, SPRING 2023

Andrew Miller, award-winning author of nine novels, was born in Bristol in 1960. He studied at Middlesex Polytechnic, University of East Anglia (with Malcolm Bradbury, Rose Tremain and Lorna Sage) and at Lancaster University, where he completed his PhD under the supervision of Professor David Craig. He has been awarded the James Tait Black Memorial Prize, the Grinzane Cavour, the International IMPAC and the Costa Book of the Year. His most recent novel, *The Slowworm's Song*, came out with Sceptre in 2022.

In April 2023 Andrew led our three-day Hothouse series of workshops, our second such series following the successful first workshop conducted by Monique Roffey in 2021. Here, selected applicants were able to join Andrew to learn from his expertise and to find support for their respective writing projects. From the cohort who joined Andrew, he has chosen David Sergeant and Sarah Mooney as his *Quay Voices*. We include a sample of each of their works here.

The Slowworm's Song

ANDREW MILLER

Morning in a room with no windows is a fairly meaningless event. I saw Corporal France slide from his bunk, lie on the floor and do press-ups. When he finished he sat on his bed, lit the day's first smoke, caught my eye and nodded. Rise, Rose.

We were lucky. We didn't have to go out at all that first day. Induction, briefings, orientation. We got some kit, including seventy-five rounds of ammunition, a mess tray and a flak jacket. The flak jackets had been bought in large numbers from the Americans at the start of the Troubles. On the tour that followed us they were issued with proper body armour, a thick ceramic plate over the heart. I don't know how much a flak jacket was ever expected to stop. Nothing serious. The one I was given was damp and smelt clearly of a man's sweat, as if he'd taken it off just a few minutes earlier, which might have been the case. Whoever it was, he'd biroed his blood group on the collar. It wasn't the same as mine (cue jokes about Welsh blood, Taffy blood) and I made sure to block it out. We queued for our issue of black Northern Ireland gloves but they ran out long before I got to the front of the queue. What they didn't run out of was yellow cards. These, which we had to carry with us at all times, stated the rules of engagement. In what circumstances you could and could not open fire, the warnings you were supposed to give (Army! Stop or I fire!). Depending on the side you were on, the card was either a license to kill or it was a legal trap, a hobble to keep us from doing our job properly. Unsurprisingly, these cards are mentioned many times in the report of the Saville Inquiry.

In the briefing room there was a map of the city that took up half a wall. Our company commander used his fly-fishing rod to point out our position, the main streets either side of us, the location of other SF bases, RUC stations, the sites of recent incidents. We were shown photographs of known or suspected terrorists. These people were called players. They were mostly young. They did not, for the most part, look sinister. And there were women too. It was strange to think they were part of it. What does it mean when even the women are against you? The Factory, of course, was full of pictures of women, hundreds of them Sellotaped to the walls of our rooms, and every sangar had its semi-secret stash of 'mags', but the women whose faces we studied in the briefing room – pictures taken at police stations or by a covert camera – stared out at us very differently. They would not be dancing with us. They were not offering themselves as the raw material of our fantasies.

And then, next morning, somewhere around five

a.m., we began in earnest. You think you won't sleep but you do. A quick wash, a scrape with a plastic razor, finish dressing, then down to the canteen. Another briefing, another look at the pictures, the arranging of call signs etc, and finally out into the air, the first hour of a summer's day, lovely even in an SF base. We loaded our weapons. Those with sights zeroed them in at the pipe-range. John France was waiting by the iron door. He checked us over and looked at his watch. There were no last-minute instructions. We either knew or we didn't. With ten seconds to go he counted down in a soft voice. We were tight as drums. Then, with a nod to the soldier acting as doorman, the door was unbolted and dragged wide.

When we left the base we always ran. A twenty-yard sprint, everything on you jangling, shifting, chafing, your breath coming hard, and all you can see somehow a source of confusion. I was the last one out. Tail-end Charlie. I stumbled as I went down the big step but did not, thank God, fall.

At the main road we slowed, checked our distances, caught our breath. A red and cream bus full of sleepy faces went by. Those who bothered to look at us did so with no obvious interest. Four more soldiers on the street, a cool morning, a scrape of moon still up. I walked, sometimes turning to walk backwards for a few paces. It did not look like Tin

City and the few people who were out were not squaddies playing civpop. Yet we seemed to understand what to do, that curious dance, slow, slow, quick-quick slow, along our route. Another bus rolled past. A man in shirt-sleeves took in his milk. I was only a few feet from him but we didn't wish each other a good morning. Some philosopher whose name I have forgotten, someone who, I think, spent time in a concentration camp, said that when you look at another person their face is saying silently, 'Please don't kill me.' I'm not sure what that man's face was saying. Quite a lot of people dealt with us by pretending we weren't there. They blanked us, and after a while that becomes quite powerful, wears away at some simple human need to be seen. But in those first minutes I wasn't bothered with any of that. I wasn't thinking about the man, his life, the life in that house. I was scanning ahead for the others, that little boat I must never get too far from, and when I saw them I pushed on, twenty-one years old, a gun in my hands, the low sun throwing my shadow ahead of me on the pavement.

That first patrol passed without incident. We saw no players. No one took a shot at us or lobbed a brick or even told us to eff off. Our route took us in a big loop towards the city centre. The worst place, the place even John France seemed nervous of, was an area of high-rises and courtyards where people lived as tightly packed as bees. A poor place even in a poor city. On the central tower there was an army observation post they resupplied by helicopter to avoid having people ambushed going up the stairs. A solid Republican area and a place we never passed through without some expectation of harm. Where we felt most exposed we ran – 'hard-targeted' – regrouping in an underpass or anywhere sheltered, anywhere it would be difficult for a gunman in one of those countless windows to settle his sights on the back of your head.

From the flats we crossed the new ring road and came to where things looked almost normal and felt safer. It wasn't, in truth, that safe. People had been killed there and the IRA regularly bombed the place as part of its economic war. But there were shops and restaurants and cafés, and while some of the names were unfamiliar, others – Boots, Woolworths, Wimpy – were not, and to see them was comforting.

For a few streets we were followed by a boy who should have been in school, a crop-haired middle-aged ten-year-old sauntering five yards behind us, hands in his pockets. Eventually, while I was hunkered down at the corner of a junction and about the same height as him, he came up and asked if I was new. He said he hadn't seen me before. How's that for cool? I think I fobbed him off with something. I probably believed my newness was a military secret, a weakness to be exploited by the boy's uncle or even by the boy himself. He stood beside me until we moved on. Having a child next to you was often thought of as a good thing, and I saw soldiers sometimes encourage their presence. Let them try on your beret, let them look through your sights. The hand holding the end of a command wire might hesitate to flick the switch if a child was there. A dead child hardly furthered the cause. In those flats we had run through, in the autumn of the year I'm talking about, INLA set off a drainpipe bomb that killed a soldier but also killed two children. The bombers were hounded out. People knew who they were, where they were hiding. They might have been lucky to get away with their lives.

We finished the patrol at an RUC station. The desk sergeant greeted us with some remark so thickly accented I couldn't understand him. We hung around in the yard of the station, glad to be hidden, then returned to the base in the back of a Humber 1 Ton truck, a vehicle known to everybody as a Pig. A quick debrief – we had nothing of official interest to report – then off to the canteen to cram our faces with the food in the trays under the heat lamps. Our first patrol! Done. Survived. Everybody had seen something strange or funny, or just *something* – the old fellow in his dressing-gown, the good-looking bird, the morning drunk singing his heart out in the underpass. We had shown our faces to the enemy. No one had messed up.

Northern Ireland? No sweat. We chattered like schoolboys. Only John France was quiet and perhaps we understood that one day we would be quiet too. We smoked, tipping our ash onto the edges of the metal plates. We drank mug after mug of over-sweetened tea. Then everyone, as if touched by the same hand, was suddenly randy for sleep and we trudged up to our room, our narrow beds with their black, wipe-down mattresses. We were QRF (quick reaction force) so we weren't allowed to take off our boots and we certainly weren't supposed to sleep but we lay down anyway, watched cartoons on the television – Rolf's Cartoon Club– then drifted and drowsed, lost ourselves in that half-world where you hear the voice of someone who's not there, a friend from boyhood, or your mum or dad calling your name. Most of my dreams in Belfast were just about Belfast. Sometimes I walked the patrol again in what felt like real time, and what I saw in the dreams was what I had seen on the streets.

Extract from *The Slowworm's Song*, Andrew Miller,
Sceptre (Hodder & Stoughton), 2022,
reprinted with permission.

Quarry

DAVID SERGEANT

The ridge curved away to the north, rearing up from the seaward plains like the spine of some archaic beast, as big as the land – the same as the land. The two men watched the banks of drizzle tearing into it from the Irish Channel, kicking up like flows in an engineer's wind tunnel. The same wind that frisked the loose folds in their jackets and nudged them sideways.

One of the men took a map out of his chest pocket. It had been pre-folded into a neat square and tremored in his hands like a nervous animal – as he peered down the slope, then up and from side to side, then back to the map and down the slope. Finally he peered sideways to his companion and nodded.

They trudged straight down off the ridge, too tired to look for a path. The wind lessened and they could hear the rustle and clump of their footsteps. Halfway down the slope was a rearing cluster of black rocks, jagged knuckles tufted with undergrowth. The first man pocketed his map and used his gloved hands to keep balance as he clambered into the peaks. The second man, though plumper, leapt onto a rock and balanced perfectly, hands still in his pockets; then leapt onto a second.

Amongst the rocks the wind was lesser still. The first man unzipped the technical-looking hood that had helmeted his face. The second man wore neither gloves nor hood but a red and green hat with a bobble. Dewdrops of rain had sewn themselves into his sandy eyebrows and the hat's fake wool.

'So this is it?' he asked.

'Definitely,' the first man told him. 'This is it.'

The second man looked around. He looked at the air, a drifting congregation of water – at the tapestry of land which came and went below – at the undulating grass. A stunted, gnarly tree of some kind had managed to find a perch here, roots snaking into the rock like the carburettor arteries of some blockbuster robot.

'There's something to it,' he said, 'I'll give you that.'

'The beginning.' The first man was already rooting around in the rock's hollows and his voice came up muffled. 'This is the start.'

The second man let this go. He did not think it was the beginning.

The first man continued to stoop and step, stoop and step, as the second man hopped from boulder to boulder above him. Then some kind of madness overtook the first man. He had been planning on finding and choosing a stone perhaps as big as his palm, something you could carry in your pocket. But everything of the last few months – years – came scurrying into his head – and with it the accusations he suspected his companion, Kent, of harbouring, that this whole endeavour was a whimsical idiocy – that Kent was feeling now a mixture of regret at being here and blame at having been led here – and the surge of anger and frustration that followed washed away all thought and it was as if the ground itself had rolled into his arms the small boulder he came up holding.

Kent's mouth popped out from his jacket.

'This one,' the first man said. 'This is just right.'

'Seriously?'

'It has to be a challenge.'

'I thought you said a stone?'

'This is a stone.'

Kent stared. 'It's a boulder.'

'What's this made of? It's a stone, it's all stone.' The first man cast around him with his head, indicating the stoniness of all the stone; he wanted to put the rock down but that would be to admit its size and weight. 'What's the point if it's not going to be a challenge?'

'Walking from the Elvis Presley Hills in Darkest Wales to Stonehenge isn't enough of a challenge?' Kent hopped closer to press home his point, effortless as a mountain goat: his agility, and the obvious resemblance of this overweight man to a mountain goat, irritated the first man. Irritated him *further*. 'Camping wild and being menaced by wolves and wankers? How many miles is it again?'

'Wolves,' the first man muttered. He had begun to lurch his burden across the grass, towards his backpack. 'I wish, wolves.'

'A colossal quantity of wankers,' Kent went on, keeping effortless pace above him. 'That's twenty-first century Britain, right? A *wilderness* of wankers. You pull up the map on your phone: *here be wankers*, it says. A hundred and seventy miles, I remember now. It's a hundred and seventy miles from here to Stonehenge. Add a few more miles for getting lost. Add a few more wankers.'

'Please stop saying *wankers*. And we're not going to get lost.'

'Of course we're going to get lost,' Kent said simply. 'A wilderness of *mad folk*, that's all I'm saying. A United Kingdom of absolute bonkers frog boxes.'

'Tell me about it,' the first man said. He gave in and put the boulder down, resting it against his chest. He could feel his heart thumping against it, irrational and persistent as a teenager's hardon. 'It's a reason to do this, though, isn't it? To get away for a bit.'

Kent looked up, towards the invisible horizon. The drizzle was lifting, the wind subsided to a steady, tidal flow. 'One reason to carry a boulder,' he said sadly.

'*I'll* carry it,' the first man snapped. 'If it's such a bother, don't worry about it. You pick a smaller rock – stone – and carry that. It doesn't matter.'

Kent looked round – affronted. 'Of course I'll

carry it. What's the point, else? A burden shared, and all that. Oh come on, Rusty, I was just surprised, that's all. But you're right, it's a challenge – not much of a story, is it, carrying a pebble in the wake of our ancestors.' He began to leap over the rocks. 'A small *megalith*, on the other hand – now that's something to tell your grandchildren about! When you have them. And they would have shared it, right, our ancestors? I mean, the burden – shared it. That was the point, you said. For the original Bluestoners.'

'Something like that,' the first man, Rusty, replied. All his energy had dissipated – and with it the rage, the frustration. 'So the research suggests.'

Kent scooped up the backpack and held it out unzipped. 'Come on then. And look, it's about the size of a football, isn't it? More or less. At its base. That'll be good, for your book.'

'A very pointy football,' Rusty objected, though his heart wasn't in it.

'And we'll erect it at Stonehenge,' Kent went on, with relish. 'All good stories end with a major erection, right?'

It was perhaps the fifteenth variety of erection joke that Kent had told since they had started out on their journey here, and Rusty felt his renewed goodwill leaking away. *Why am I always so angry?* a voice in his head addressed him – a strange voice, his own, but summoned out of some unsuspected quarter so it felt like it was not quite him. The image of Michelle succeeded the voice, an image radiating guilt and love. Suddenly he missed her, with all his heart, and the journey was worthwhile, if only to feel that – worthwhile and misconceived, a pointless, belated penance.

'Easy,' Kent muttered, rocking the fabric of the bag around the boulder – like a reverse birth, squeezing a pelvis back over a baby's too-big head. 'Easy – right, shove – there, mm. How's that?'

The bag was just wide enough to take the rock. Rusty heaved it onto his back and suppressed the groan that followed. He thought of his gear, ultralightweight camping equipment assembled at considerable expense and lined up on the bedroom floor of a cottage that lay somewhere in the mist below. Despite its high-tech materials, the gear had managed to seem oppressively heavy when he had packed it all together for the first time. And now, the rock on top.

'This is probably illegal,' he said. 'Ancient monuments. We're looting a site of national significance.'

Kent squinted into the desolation of mist – the jagged tors – the blank repeating grass. 'And yet, just maybe it will survive our visit. Shall I take a turn?'

'I haven't started yet.'

'Alright. Say when you want me to take a turn.'

At the foot of the slope the plain of inland

Pembrokeshire was laid out before them – or would have been if it weren't for the weather – and beyond it land, and land, and more land, all the way round to Salisbury Plain. Rusty closed his eyes. It was as if he had not properly realized what he had embarked upon till now, for all that he could visualize every section of the map.

'You can play me in, like.' Kent came up to his shoulder. 'Pass the ball off, the pointy ball. Just like the old days.'

Rusty looked round, and it was like he was seeing Kent for the first time. Shiny face, rose-red cheeks, eyebrows and lashes threaded with dew, and over or through it all some kind of pulsating network of light.

He found himself saying: 'I wonder what Colin would have made of this.'

Kent laughed. 'Can't you see him? He would have raised his eyebrows – like this – and then: *what in the name of jiggery buttons are you two doing out here? Daft badgers.*' He caught sight of Rusty's expression. 'Well – you can't say he wouldn't.'

Rusty did not reply, but hefted the straps again on his shoulders and started downhill.

Extract from *The Bluestone Path*,
David Sergeant

Summoned

SARAH MOONEY

Julia dragged her school bag and her feet towards the head's office. The heavy wooden door was ajar. The slight openness was something the head had learnt in one of her management training courses to make her seem more approachable. Julia knocked with one hand and pushed it with the other, suddenly feeling confused and uncertain…should she have waited even though it was open? Did she need to knock? Should she have walked straight in? Her brain was thinking itself into a stupor when the head spoke, 'Come in.'

Julia hovered at the door for a moment, her body resisting the threshold into the head's office. It smelt of dust and bleach, and Julia marvelled that there was room for both smells to be in the air and go up her nose. She felt sure one should cancel the other out but she sniffed again, unmistakeable.

'Come in,' the voice repeated, jerking Julia out of her nose and into the room.

Ms Arident was looking down as she entered so she looked around. There was a vast bookshelf. Julia could see that most of the spines of the leather-bound books were uncracked, which meant unread. There were trophies dotted about too. Jules hoped for a ridiculous moment that she was being called in to be presented with a trophy for some race she had entered and won without realising it.

Julia's eyes continued around the room, noticing the squareness of it all, desk, tables, books, even the lamp on the table was long and oblong. She noticed that Ms Arident's face had the same longness to it. She was just transposing her features onto a potato in her mind (whenever she thought the word head, she always put the word potato in front of it) when the head looked straight at her. Julia instantly looked at her feet, where she saw that one of her socks had worked its way down past her ankle and almost under her foot.

'I am sorry for your loss.'

Julia looked up, shocked. She thought the head (potato) was talking about her sock but then the cement of feeling crashed through her brain fudge and she felt the leaden weight of mourning fill her.

'I am, er, thanks…'

Julia may have said something else. The head may have said something like, 'Fwa fwa fwa fwa fwa.' But they both, for this moment, had burning sensations in their ears (maybe someone was thinking about them, perhaps it was because they were thinking about each other).

Sounds were muffled and confused. There was a pause, long enough to establish that neither of them was talking and the head jumped in.

'Moving forward...'

They both let out a sigh, they had made it through the awkward part of the conversation and on to the practical.

Julia nodded eagerly, then felt stupid at letting this dry old crust see how desperate to please she was.

'As we are two weeks away from half term, and due to your situation' – the head had meant to say circumstance but it had gone awry on her tongue – 'some of your behaviour has been, curious...so after your father's funeral...the school has decided...'

Julia could almost hear the wrought iron gates of the school entrance sliding between them.

The head coughed, a sort of choking strangle of a sound before she finished her sentence.

'You do not need to return immediately.'

An image flashed through Ms Arident's eyes: an unpacked suitcase, locked tight shut. It was where she put all her uncomfortable feelings, it made her able to rule the school. This girl in front of her seemed to have no such thing. Her feelings seemed to leak all over her face, her desk, her pencil case...they just simply could not have it, not at her school.

'We have decided to give you until the end of the break to, er, grieve...then come back dry eyed and ready to knuckle down and learn.'

Julia had not cried. She was cracker dry, as dry as

this lizard in the desert of her desk. Now she slumped, wanting to sit in the leather chair in front of her but not quite daring too, settling for using it as an ornate Zimmer frame. Three weeks to eat through the days like a caterpillar, cry all her tears and come back transformed.

She wondered if she would get a trophy for that.

Sniffing the Moor

The day was fresh, mizzy. Spinner was wandering the moors, closer to the road than she would like to be but a twitchy feeling had brought her here. Jubilantly she noticed a snowdrop dangling above the ground, its head held forward. She looked around and saw moss-covered rock and a cobweb jewelled with morning water. She knew this was the place. Standing up, she made her prayers to the four directions so that her spinning did not snag. She looked again at the spider's web. Always good to be close to a spider, a creature that spins from the centre of her very being...that was how it felt for Spinner too, like it was all connected to her guts. It was a wind whipping, sun shining sort of a day and by Boudicca it was good to get out of the caves and into the fresh air of the moor. She shook the feeling of dampness and the smelly staleness from her skirts and took her hand-held bobbin out of her pocket. The bobbin had been put in her cradle as a baby. It was made of wood, about six inches long and smooth as silk from the generations of women's hands that had held and wound it. Her family had always been Spinners, walking the land to collect what had been discarded and re-spinning it back into the world. Of course, she could spin wildflower and damp moss, no problem, but with her spindle held just right she could catch a bird song or lover's sigh and that was the magic of it. It was a knack of knowing what to spin and how to spin it, a just-right feeling on the inside. She leant towards the flower and held her bobbin next to the snowdrop's birth caul, she was not spinning the flower itself but the whisper of tenacity that still surrounded it as it made its journey through the cold earth. It made a faint whooshing sound as it spun onto her bobbin. When Spinner was confident that she had all of it (tenacity was such a tender thread and so often snapped) she lifted the bobbin up to the sun and then quickly down to touch the earth as she had been taught by her grandmothers and aunties.

She was about to return the bobbin to her pocket when she heard a coppery sound and saw a strand of something glistening in the bush. She took a few steps forward and saw it was a hair. At first she thought it was a windblown, blackthorn-caught horse hair... Weaver would be pleased with that. It would have swiftness of horse *and* speed of wind within it. Weaver could do a lot with that. Spinner expertly catches the hair between her fingers and connects it to the bobbin, and as she does so she sees it is a human hair. As it winds around the bobbin it sparkles and crackles.

'It's her!' she exclaims, nodding around to rock and bush. 'Her!'

Spinner runs, trips and nearly drops the bobbin, stops, places the bobbin ever so carefully into her pocket then continues running.

She reaches a great manor house but runs straight past the front gate and around the side of the house, streaking past a garden once prized for its topiary, now wild and dishevelled. There is a stone fountain and more garden but then the human-made landscape drops away and there is water bubbling up from underground and a cave mouth. Spinner hauls an old wooden boat out from where she had left it behind a jutting rock, and punts her way into the depths of the cave.

JANE ELSON

SHORT COURSE TUTOR, AUTUMN 2022

After performing as an actress and comedy improviser, Jane fell into writing stories and plays. Her books have won many literary awards including Peters Book of the Year two years running. Her debut novel, *A Room Full of Chocolate*, was longlisted for the Branford Boase Award and she has twice been nominated for the Carnegie Medal.

Jane is loud and proud about her dyslexia and over the years has mentored many neurodiverse young people, promoting the gift of alternative thinking. She was honoured to be named as one of the Top 50 Influential Neurodivergent Women by Women Beyond The Box. Jane's niche in the market is writing about those children who are often not written about. In her latest book, *Storm Horse*, Jane returns to the world of the Beckham Estate, also featured in the multi-award-winning *How to Fly with Broken Wings* and *Will You Catch Me?*

Jane is a trustee for the charity NACoA and wrote *Lockdown Nell* featuring Nell from *Will You Catch Me?* to encourage children trapped with alcohol-dependent parents during the pandemic to phone NACoA's helpline.

For Quay Words Jane led a five-week short course on Writing Children's Fiction. Of those who joined Jane on her course, she has chosen Dawn Amesbury and Melissa Boyce-Hurd as her *Quay Voices*.

Storm Horse

JANE ELSON

In the Beginning

My great-great-grandad, Cuthbert H. Brown Junior, lived in a car. His ma slept in the front seat, his pa in the driving seat and Cuthbert H. Brown Junior, who was small like me, curled up on the back seat with his sister Dora and brother Frank – all higgledy-piggledy with their pots and pans and clothes.

When it was warm, they slept on the grass, looking up at the night sky, sending the stars wishes that they could get rich and live in a house again.

Because, you see, my American ancestors – that's why I said ma and pa (like old-time American films) – well, they lost everything, along with thousands of people, in what they called the Great Depression, and they often went to sleep with rumbling bellies.

Sometimes it's a bit like that for me, Daniel Margate, and some of the other kids on the Beckham Estate where I live in north-west London. Two whole months and a week ago, Mum and me and my little brother Jackson went on one of our visits to the food bank 'cause Mum had nothing in her purse to feed us with. When we reached the bit of the table with the pasta, Jackson flung himself out of his buggy onto the floor and screamed loud enough to shatter windows and Mum couldn't make him stop and started crying too. I curled up in a ball in the corner with my fingers in my ears. Then a lady called Jackie gave me a hot chocolate and a Jammie Dodger biscuit and Mum a hug and everything was all right again for two and a half minutes till Jackson started screaming again.

Anyway, back to the story I was telling you about. One day Cuthbert H. Brown Junior's pa used their last bit of gasoline (what we call petrol) and drove the car that they lived in all the way to a racecourse, to see the horse Seabiscuit race the great War Admiral.

Cuthbert H. Brown Junior's pa, Cuthbert H. Brown Senior – who was my great-great-great-grandfather – lifted him high onto his shoulders to watch Seabiscuit win in the most exciting race ever and the crowd went wild and their hearts felt mended again and they had hope. You see, Seabiscuit was too small to be a racehorse. He had knobbly knees, stubby legs and walked funny, swinging a foreleg out as he went. He captured the hearts of all the broken people who had lost their money in the Great Depression, thinking maybe they could be winners too one day.

This true story of Seabiscuit the racehorse from long ago gives me hope. Sometimes when it's dark I go outside and look up and I imagine Seabiscuit riding across the night sky. After the screaming incident in the food bank, I sneaked out of my flat and I went all the way up to the eighteenth floor of the Beckham Estate and up, up onto the roof (where we are not allowed to go), so that I would be nearer the night sky and feel closer to Seabiscuit as he raced through the stars. I held up my hands to my hero horse and made a wish. I swear Seabiscuit heard 'cause the very next week my mum got a job at the Beckham Animal Rescue Centre.

I said thank you to Seabiscuit, and saved three weeks' pocket money and bought lots of packets of Jammie Dodgers to take down to Jackie at the food bank for the other hungry kids.

'Thank you for your kindness,' she said and her eyes watered up. I know that Molly-May from my Silver Reading Group at school is always starving. I've seen her come out of the food bank with her dad. I hope Jackie gives her lots of biscuits. Whenever I've got enough money in my pocket I buy a packet of Jammie Dodgers to keep in my school bag for emergencies.

I dream about Seabiscuit a lot: the racehorse who was too small, ridden by Red Pollard, a jockey who was too tall. [A jockey is the person what rides a racehorse.] Red Pollard had red hair like me, he carried a bundle of treasured books wherever he went, and walked around quoting Shakespeare to the other jockeys, saying things like 'O for a horse with wings!'

Red Pollard could read really well, but as for me — well, I just can't. When I try to read, the words get all jumbled and move all over the place. This is 'cause I'm dyslexic.

I wish I was Red Pollard, not Daniel Margate.

From *Storm Horse*, Jane Elson,
Hodder Children's Books, 2021,
reprinted with permission.

The Withered Man

MELISSA BOYCE-HURD

The withered man shuffled amongst the shadows in his dark house, as if he were one of them, before slumping down into a ripped armchair with a sharp intake of breath and a creaking of limbs. He stared intently at the stained carpet beneath his feet and then turned to the sofa across from him.

'What's the time, dear?'

The woman opposite him glowed golden in the late afternoon sunlight. She frowned up from the book she was clutching in her hands.

'Darling, there's a clock above my head.' And she returned to her book.

'Oh, yes…' He raised his gaze to the shattered, motionless clock propped atop the doorframe. 'My! Already? I need to go and fetch the children!' He made to stand up, but fell back into his chair with a grunt of exhaustion.

The woman observed him, then asked cautiously, 'The children…from where?'

He looked pensively into the gloomy corners of the room.

'The kids aren't at school, darling.' She added, 'The kids don't go to school anymore…'

'Why? Are they ill?'

'The kids are all grown up remember?' she asked softly.

'What?'

'Well, Joshua moved to Germany and…' She continued warily as the aged man's face began to crease with uncertainty, 'Martha got married. You're a grandfather…you remember.'

His frown turned to a grin and he chuckled to himself. 'A grandfather. You always knew how to make me laugh. I really believed you there for…' But then he stopped and scratched his chin. Abruptly his tired eyes turned to liquid sadness and he looked away from her.

'It's OK. You just forgot.' She put down her book.

He watched her for a while. 'But how could I?' he asked eventually.

'We all forget things, darling.' She bit her lip and avoided his eyes.

Then his eyes filled with terror and his fingers grappled instinctively with the armrests beneath them. 'Germany?' he almost shrieked. 'But my boy's not safe there! He can't fight!' He writhed in his seat as muffled words caught in his throat. 'He's too young. Get him home! Let them take me instead.' He had begun to sob, yet still the words poured out like his tears, 'My leg's healed…only a scar from the bullet now. Let me go in his place.'

The woman hushed him to calm his nerves. 'No, no darling. He's safe there now. That's all over. He's safe.'

'You don't know that!' His sobs turned to spittle and snarls, 'You don't know he'll make it out alive! And if he does, you couldn't understand the horror… the nightmares…flashes of fire that burn in your eyes even now, the putrid smell of burnt flesh, the things terror will drive you…'

'No, that's all over now. It's only bad dreams and painful memories now. I promise…' Her words soothed him and his shouting stopped.

When the horrified flicker in his eyes had died down and his grip had loosened from the battered armrests, he sighed and blinked rapidly as if clearing all the remains of tormenting images from his eyes. 'How's the bookshop doing without me?' he asked her suddenly.

She winced and her eyes fell to the carpet.

'I need to rearrange the shelf by the window when I get back.'

'You aren't going back.' She gazed at him pityingly. 'You can't.'

'What? Why ever not?'

She clenched her jaw as if trying to swallow something sickening and told him, 'Because you sold the bookshop.'

He looked at her, confused. 'I'd never sell the bookshop. That place…means the world to me.' He smiled at the wall. 'The smell of paper.' His eyes became dazed as if he were reciting a poem, 'The echoes of words once read, the anticipation of those you've yet to read.'

She smiled sadly, like she'd heard it all before.

'I'd never give that up,' he huffed, reassured by his own words, only to be broken by hers.

'The old bookshop on the top of the hill.' Her smile deepened at the memory, 'With a rooftop covered in tiny flowers like tassels in someone's hair. Where children came for adventures and adults came to escape.' Her eyes sparkled with wonder, then with tears. 'But you sold it when the walk up the hill was too far and the boxes of books were too heavy.'

He started to cry as it all came back. 'I didn't want to. I never…never wanted to. I didn't have a choice.'

'I know.' She smiled at him through watery eyes.

They sat in silence as he remembered. Finally, he asked, 'Do you remember when we first met?'

'Of course.'

'I…I thought you told me you'd forgotten.'

'No. Never.' Nostalgia appeared to overcome her as she reminisced, 'In the very same bookshop on a warm summer's evening…'

'But, lingering on the breeze…the smell of autumn in the air.'

'And I saw you, by the bookshelf through the window, and then I came in.'

'And you asked me for a book on the top shelf.'

'*Great Expectations*,' she muttered, 'I always loved that book.'

'And I knocked over the entire shelf in my hurry to help you.' They both laughed together.

'Then,' she continued, 'we spent the rest of the evening reading and talking to each other until we fell asleep in the bookshop's armchairs.' She stared into nothingness with the ghost of a smile playing on her lips. The old man looked at his wife. Her raven-black curls rolled over her shoulders and her ruby-red lips were still parted in a smile. The sunlight glittered off the turquoise pleats in the cotton of her dress as she wrung her smooth hands distractedly in her lap. She glanced up at him.

'I love you,' he told her. But she didn't hear him. She didn't see him sitting there in the all-devouring darkness of the decomposing room. She would never see or hear him again. But he heard her say, 'I love you, too,' so he smiled contentedly at the empty sofa opposite him.

Village of Spies

DAWN AMESBURY

Chapter One
Thorp Arch, Yorkshire

8th June 1940

I wish I hadn't answered the door that day. I wish I hadn't been home at all.

On a normal Saturday there'd have been Mum, and I'd have been halfway to the pictures. But it was siling it down and Henry had gone AWOL. As I dashed back for my coat and boots, Mum ran off to look for him.

Of course, it wouldn't have changed anything – being at home I mean, not the fact I was wearing a coat. Because death, well, you can't escape it, especially now. And there's never a good way to hear that news, even when it's someone you hated, someone you wished would never come back.

My throat was so tight I could only nod my thanks to the messenger boy. I watched him cycle away through the curtains of rain, telegram flapping in my hand like a wounded bird.

I closed the door in a daze and wandered around the hall, the kitchen, the sitting room. There was nothing of his in these rooms, yet, somehow, I could almost see him in his uniform, smell the tobacco of his pipe.

The walls closed in and I fought to steady my breath. I had to get out of here – not just the house, this whole place. All the years we'd put up with the whispers, the gossip, the pitying looks…

I left the telegram on the hall table. I wouldn't wait for Mum; I couldn't face seeing her cry. Anger and guilt welled up inside me. This, on top of all the grief we'd had to deal with, was just too much.

As I dashed from the house, the rain mushroomed over my brolly, turning me into one of those fountain statues. Water hammered the pavement and streamed down the road. Then I went and put my foot in a hole and muck splattered all over my coat. Mum would be so mad she'd make *me* wash it this time.

I was soaked through and filthy, but there was no way I was going home. My life was rotten, but once a week I had the chance to escape it all, and I wasn't giving that up for anything. I splashed through the churchyard, reaching the stop just as the bus arrived.

* * *

The walk from the bus stop was just as wet and, of course, the picture house queue was a mile long. I willed it to move faster, but the queue inched forwards and I spent a lifetime staring at the backs in front of me. But, rain or no rain, I had to wait. I hadn't missed a single week in three years; I'd seen every George Formby film and I wasn't about to miss this one. He was so daft that, even on my worst day, he could cheer me up.

The queue buzzed; dozens of damp young teens and twenty-somethings chatting and laughing with friends, boyfriends and girlfriends. For three years I'd come here alone. But once I was inside it didn't matter – in the dark no one noticed you. And once the first feature started I could leave my life behind and live someone else's…

Two soldiers waved from over the road to three giggling girls who called out and waved back.

Soldiers…*the telegram*…oh God, Mum must have seen it by now. I shouldn't have left it on the table, but I couldn't face…

Suddenly the queue moved and I was right by the picture house doors, under the canopy. Nice, but I couldn't have got much wetter. I'd had plenty of soakings outside this place though, and it was always worth it. Only this and detective books made life bearable. So, unless the Germans bombed this place, nothing would stop me coming here.

At last I was inside and bought my ticket from the booth. An usherette, not much older than me, used a torch to show us to our seats through the thick fug of smoke.

I ended up squashed between a large lady and a courting couple, but I was *here* and that was all that mattered. I fumbled in my pocket for the brown paper bag; it had come apart, but the sweets were still there. As we waited for the first feature I unwrapped one and let the sweetness spread over my tongue. *Everything would be fine.*

The screen lit up, people shushed each other, then it was all munching and rustling.

'Pathé News' and a crowing cockerel flashed onto the screen. *Oh God, the newsreel!* I wanted to escape the war, not hear more about it. But I was sandwiched in and it was right there on the big screen. Soldiers staggered off boats, dazed, dirty and tired. Some were bandaged, some leant on fellow soldiers as they struggled to walk. Some were carried on stretchers. Battered, bruised and bloody, but alive: the lucky ones.

A posh man's voice jabbered on about our valiant soldiers and the brave little boat owners who had answered Churchill's call. He went on and on about how many men had been saved. It was a miracle, he said, but he didn't say a word about the ones left behind.

My eyes blurred and there they were: hundreds of soldiers trapped on the beach, bombs and bullets everywhere. Hell on earth. Blown to bits before they could be rescued. Never seeing their families and friends again. What about *them*? The newsreel didn't mention *them*.

My stomach lurched so bad I spat the sweet into my hand, clenched my fist around it and fought the urge to yell: 'Show us what *really* happened! Stop saying it's a success and *tell us the truth!*'

But the usherette would've got me thrown out and I couldn't bear not coming here again. Life was bad enough.

I took some deep breaths. In…out…in…out…but all the smoke made me cough.

The newsreel ended and on came a stupid Popeye cartoon. And because he was a sailor on a boat, my mind wandered back to the men on that horrible beach.

At last the cartoon ended and the credits began to roll for *Come on, George. About bloomin' time!* I'd been waiting months to see this. George Formby was great *and* he was northern, although from the wrong side of the Pennines (as Gran used to say).

The film started with everyone at the races; a horse owner was yelling at his jockey, telling him to whip his horse to make him go faster. The horse threw its rider at the third fence and it served him right. If only bullies got their come-uppance in real life.

George was a gormless ice cream seller. As always, he got straight into bother, accidentally ending up with a stolen wallet. Then it turned into a crazy chase, with George causing mayhem with his ice cream cart. When George knocked everyone over, the woman next to me howled with laughter and yet I couldn't manage a smile.

The darkness and smoke closed in, choking me. The picture blurred and I was back on my doorstep, telegram flapping, trying to speak. The messenger boy's sorry face. The pain. The unbearable pain...

Watch the damn film and stop him from ruining your life anymore – he's gone and he's not coming back. *Isn't that what you wanted?*

And there was George, being chased around a railway station. George running on top of a moving train with a tunnel approaching. George jumping into the horsebox just in time. George being tricked into looking after a 'deadly' horse called Maneater. George playing a song to the horse. It got sillier and sillier. The large woman shrieked with laughter and the young couple giggled non-stop. I stared through the screen, barely breathing.

If we won the war, would his name be carved into a memorial? Would people say nice things about him? Funny how someone has to die before everyone says how great they were. Maybe when I die people will say nice things about me.

But first I wanted a good life, which could never happen here. I might be only fourteen, but with the right clothes, hair and makeup, I could pass for older.

I could move somewhere else, start again. All I needed was a job…

Henry's grinning, freckled face popped into my head. I swallowed hard – he'll be fine, he's got Mum and his mates – *flippin' 'eck he's ten* – I'll write to him every week. And I'll make sure whatever I do and wherever I go will be worth writing about.

YOUNG VOICES

TRADING PLACES FLASH FICTION WRITING COMPETITION

For a third year, Quay Words' successful competition for young writers invited young people aged 14–18 years to write a piece of short or 'flash' fiction: up to 250 words for those aged 14–18 and up to 500 words for those aged 10–14. We continued the theme of 'Trading Places', which fits so well with the trading heritage of Quay Words' location and opens up such imaginative potential. This year's winners surprised the judges with their wit and originality. Congratulations to Violet, Meggie and Mitchel (14–18 years category) and to Emily, Inigo and Scarlett (10–14 years category); and thanks too, to everyone who entered such well-written and entertaining compositions.

Trading Places: Flash Fiction

Category: 14–18 Years of Age

FIRST PLACE

Mother and Daughter, Violet Stapleton (*age 16*)

Red wine spills on the floor, bleeding into the carpet. She cuts her foot on the glass. Later, I patch it up as she leans into the sofa, stars swimming around her head. I look to her as if she is a goddess, and she looks through me like I'm an apparition. I am desperate for her warmth. She is a relic of war; I can almost see the fingerprints on her, feel the bruises in her quiet. On weekdays, she sits in the conservatory and soaks up sun. It's the only time I see her shoulders slump.

Mother and I, though I feel like more of the former these days.

I fall asleep over homework. There is something hollow about me. I am afraid one day someone will reach in and there will be nothing there.

Second Place

Brave, Meggie Lenn (*age 15*)

She lives in my head. I see her every night as I lie under the protection of the stars and the moon. I see her when my eyes are squeezed tight shut. I see her, but nobody else can.

Strong and fierce. My eyes survey her intense dimensions and complexity. I'm still mesmerised after all this time. From the ivory pigment of her skin to the rays of sun trapped between her golden curls. She breathes freedom and liberation. The feeling of home. The most beautiful miracle.

The criss-cross creases on her face bloom into maps and stories. Her laugh is an enchanting song of hope. She holds the knowledge of the universe – it flows through her. She guides me and advises me. She always has.

Every time I close my eyes, make a wish. I wish that she would find a way out of the cage that is my mind. There's no space for her up there. It's too full. I fantasise about the time when I will be her and she will be me, the day when we will trade places. I'm torn between the urge to hide her and the desire to show her off to the world.

I look into the mirror and see her reflected back at me. I live a double life. She's always there and always will be. She is me. Or at least she will be, when I'm brave enough to let her out.

THIRD PLACE

A Twenty-First Century Suburban Dream, Mitchel Rowe (*age 18*)

I glimpsed her through a slit in our flaking banister, lured by a song she'd implored to be played on the day of her funeral. There she was, my mother, after everyone had returned home. Her body was smashed into the embrace of the old family sofa, lying there sedated, eyes rolling back to heaven. Her nails painted with the chipped ecstasy of one-too-many, Dad had hollered, nearly broken down the door in the thick of the party. I'd only gone down to use the bathroom, or so I said. But seeing her crumpled white dress, lipstick that had smeared across her, cheek-to-cheek, I couldn't not go in. I stepped quietly, just looking at her body, sort of detached, while some drug-drowned soul-star slurred a heavy melody that hid me away until I was brave enough to enter.

'Mum, you OK?' She stirred quickly. I seemed to plough her out of wherever she'd been.

'Oh, hello——' she said, vague and far away as her eyes came to meet mine. 'Lie with me. Give me a hug.'

'Oh, no. I just wanted to make sure you were, you know, OK?'

'Come on.'

And she made space. I sighed, gave in. Though once I lay next to her, I became aware that flies had breached our house on this warm summer's evening. First one, then another. On her thighs, in her hair, she didn't even notice. And as she hummed along to the music, I wafted them away, thinking, *not now, not yet.*

Trading Places: Flash Fiction

Category: 10-14 years of age

FIRST PLACE

The Wizard and the Cat, Emily Harvey (*age 12*)

Growing bored of listening to the old wizard shouting, I walked off. He was always shouting nowadays – always yelling at me to leave the stupid-looking bird alone. Apparently, it was a 'special endangered creature'. To me it's just a pest who shouldn't be in my house.

I started cleaning my golden and brown, thick, silky fur and I saw it: the large red and yellow bird, the thing I hated most. The thing I could torment and chase. I leapt for it, digging my claws into its sides. Hearing it squawking in distress and pain was music to my ears. I felt the wizard's disapproving stare behind me, so I looked around. He was scowling. Not shouting, not screaming, but scowling. I let go of the bird, confusion flooding my mind like water through a broken dam.

Why wasn't he shouting? Was I in trouble? No, that couldn't be right. Me, descendant of the mighty lion, regal and glorious, couldn't be in trouble. Just when I came to that conclusion, the wizard lowered the big log that he always carried around and pointed it at me. Bam! With a massive blue flash, everything went dark.

Slowly awakening, I sleepily opened my eyes, looked down and saw a crimson colour instead of brown. I blinked and blinked again but there were still crimson and gold feathers where my gorgeous fur should be. I could see my paws were talons; my legs were skinny and scaly looking and at the end of what should have been my snout was a hooked beak. It was then that I realised that foolish old wizard had turned me into the repulsive feather duster he called a bird.

Anger rushed through my veins at the thought that the stupid flying vermin was probably right now enjoying being in my majestic, royal, fabulous, luxurious, gorgeous and fantastic body. Then, the realisation hit me as if I had run headfirst into a solid brick wall. If I had been able to claw, chase and torture it, wouldn't it now be able to scratch, claw, chase and torture me?

Suddenly, I heard the pit patter of a cat. Coming ever closer, I saw my old, beautiful body plod over, a smile of pure happiness on its face. I stood there, frozen with fear, unable to move.

SECOND PLACE

Nature Drifts, Inigo Quinlivan-Brewer (*age 10*)

Dust floating down the lane. I am a tiny particle of pollen inside an enormous dandelion. There are bits of light like feathers moving around me. The hay baler is a hurricane. I move around the barley fields and find a home below the wings of a bee. Sweet and spongy with golden patches, like a lightbulb in my house in Devon.

THIRD PLACE

A Whisper to the World, Scarlett Fox (*age 10*)

One sunny evening Betty was walking with her friend Alice in town. They were chewing gum and heading to the sweet shop.

'Hey, would you like to get some more gum? I heard they are doing a new flavour, it's called lemon fizz or something like that,' said Alice.

'Sure, OK,' said Betty.

Just then Alice spat the gum she had been chewing out onto the pavement and said, 'Hey, have you seen the new picture that Matt posted on the group chat? He has a new puppy, a Doberman, I think.' As they looked through their text messages, they crossed the road and…BANG!

All went black.

Betty's life had ended…

Or had it?

Betty found herself flying. For her life now was the life of a swallow.

It was amazing to be able to fly and feel the wind through her feathers; dipping and diving through the town and the park. She discovered a whole new world around her that she had never noticed as a human.

One morning while Betty was flying, she came across a familiar place. And there she noticed a small robin who was choking on some gum. Betty realised it was the same gum that Alice had spat out. Sadly the robin could not be saved.

High up in one of the oak trees, Betty also discovered that the robin had left four hungry chicks behind who were tweeting away and waiting for their mother to return.

So over the next few weeks Betty tended to the chicks and very soon they grew to be beautiful young robins.

SOPHIE DUMONT

WRITER-IN-RESIDENCE, SUMMER 2022

Sophie Dumont is a poet, copywriter and ex-canoe coach living in Bristol. She is an alumna of Exeter University and her poetry has been published widely, including in *The Rialto*. Sophie won the Brian Dempsey Memorial Prize 2021, came third in this year's Magma Poetry Competition and has been shortlisted for the Bridport Prize twice.

Sophie's poetry is anchored in themes of urban waterways as she explores her relationship to bodies of water and what the river can carry. Sophie completed a Creative Writing MA at Bath Spa University and was awarded a poetry residency along Bristol Harbourside through Boat Poets. She has written three immersive productions for Riptide, a Leeds-based theatre company. The latest production, *SONDER*, is an app experience using GPS satellite navigation and a 360° binaural sound walk along the River Aire in Leeds. Her website is sophiedumont.co.uk.

Sophie's residency at Quay Words coincided with our 'Maritime' season. She explored and researched Exeter's maritime past and took inspiration from people still using watercraft on the river. Her poem 'Index to Exeter Quay/From the Blue Door I Beckon' was created during her residency. From those who joined Sophie during her residency, she has selected *Quay Voices* Lou Jones and Heidi Stephenson.

Index of Exeter Quay From the Blue Door I Beckon

SOPHIE DUMONT

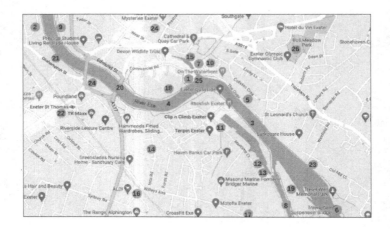

1. It's here that I first read: Exeter is considered to have lost its route to the sea.

2. A woman is wearing The Great Wave Off Kanagawa as a mask over her mouth.

3. Kayakers dig all morning and leave no trace of what they've moved.

4. For *river*, see *mirror*.

5. I bought a ceramic bowl, fired with a glass nugget

within it to create the effect of a pool of water constantly at its base.

6. There's a fire extinguisher lodged in the weir. See also >> shoes, traffic cone, water's memory of moor.

7. It's the hottest summer on record and tap water is the same temperature as inside a mouth, or kissing. I return each week to the blue door of the Custom House, watch the mirage of this water.

8. I canoe to find Countess Wear, the suburb containing the weir built by the 7th Countess of Devon in 1284 to block Exeter's thriving port. No one knows where the weir is; the Exe swallowed it whole: an *archaeological dilemma*.

9. I replace my notebook with a sketchbook. I collage a river and use only ripped pieces of sky.

10. This porch was Elizabeth Dock 400 years ago, used for small barges to offload larger ships, too big to come into the wharf. The dock is now inland, is now a menu of ice creams, a chiropractor with the original mooring rings on the shop's front.

10a. I remember sheltering under this canopy, 1am, breathing vodka and coke ghosts into the night, the club pulsing next door. The rain was so heavy it wiped each second clean. I stood on what I now know to have been river and pulled someone in closer. The rain spilled down the stairs to meet us at river level, returning to its former self as I lost mine.

11. Hulled things: upturned palms, pockets, a middle name.

12. A group of girls in life jackets crouch to touch the river, in anticipation of falling in – like a mother's hand gauging a forehead.

13. For *sisterhood*, stay here.

14. I read a tweet stating that house martins don't drink water off the ground – only that which is suspended.

15. A girl in a workshop tells me she will describe these windows as mouths.

16. Ick = river creek, cow creek, watering place.

17. Black Thursday, 1960. So much rain it burst the banks and, for a brief period, Exeter was cut off from the country. At what point does river become sea?

18. I've noticed the fierce heat has me speaking in eddies, in circling pools.

19. The Spillway – a section built especially for the spilling.

20. My sister calls, holds the phone up to show me my five-year-old niece in an iridescent leotard. She

has just learnt to do a bridge at gymnastics. I hold my phone up so that my niece's body arches over the Exe.

21. I dunk my cookie into weak tea, notice the eels writhe in the cornicing.

22. I remember walking home from school after the flood. The water was up to here. She slides her hand under her chin – throat height.

22a. My mother nearly bought that house. There's a mark across the wall where the river pushed itself against the sofa, licked at the paintwork. You can't get a watermark out of plaster.

23, 24, 25. (Buddleia).

26. I phone my sister, tell her of my recurring dream: I wake in a flooded house. The moon has lit a path for the sea to rage up the spine of the Exe. I walk slowly downstairs, returning myself with each cold step. River rises up me like it does to the wall in a lock, I say, it rises up me like light.

The Enigma

LOU JONES

Heron stock-still
Enigma
Good talisman
We see you. Do you see us?

Heron stealthy stabber
Hunting
Water dancer
How deep do you see? Only fish?

Lofty lone ranger
Launching
Jurassic flyer
What do you see? Just a river?

Slipping back to your heronry, beyond the turf
Vanished into tree folds.

Heaven in Devon

HEIDI STEPHENSON

Sheep shorn *sharply*:
Devon lambs and ewes!

Tenterhooks and tillet blocks.

Cricklepit Mill merchants
Made rich through *fleecing*.

Ships loaded with stained wool
cloth for the tidal gold rush.

Rising fortunes, from the fallen…

Trading in 'goods', in the ebb
And flow of *life*-blood.

Death cult revenue.

Unidentified, bobbing subject:
Washed up, would-be shore settler.

War-torn, barnacle baby drifting…
'When the boat comes in…'

Uncomprehending milk eyes frozen,
(never to spawn foreign dreams).

The cold waves roll, open-armed;
less crowded now (so room-a-plenty).

Thanks to overfishing, city greed, killing quotas,
and an ever dwindling respect for *life*:

'You shall have a fishy on a little dishy…'

Watery conscience too late,
to save your days.

MARTYN WAITES

Short Course Tutor, Summer 2022

Martyn Waites was born in Newcastle Upon Tyne. He trained at the Birmingham School of Speech and Drama and worked as an actor for many years before becoming a writer. His novels include the critically acclaimed Joe Donovan series set in the North East and *The White Room* which was a *Guardian* book of the year. In 2013 he was chosen to write *Angel of Death*, the official sequel to Susan Hill's *The Woman in Black*, and in 2014 won the Grand Prix du Roman Noir for *Born under Punches*. He has been nominated for every major British crime fiction award and has enjoyed international commercial success with eight novels written under the name of Tania Carver. He lives in Exeter.

In summer 2022, Martyn taught a short course for Quay Words on Writing Crime Fiction. The excerpt from Martyn's work we include here is from his latest novel, published by Blackstone Publishing in 2022. Of those who joined Martyn's course, he has selected Jolyon Tuck and Sarah Fox as his *Quay Voices*.

Gravedigger's Song

MARTYN WAITES

Along the lane they came. Punch and Judy at the front, Turnip Head leading the Horse by the reins. None spoke. None needed to.

The night was clear and bone cold, black winter ascendant. No stars, the moon distant, cloud-imprisoned. The trees and bushes on either side were deep, unyielding. Their shadows and hollows black doorways into underworlds of uncertain mud, moss, stone, and spiked branches.

The four knew the route. Every turn, hidden sinkhole, bog of no return. Every wayward meandering trail. Light or dark didn't matter. This was their home. Their land.

The bell on Mr Punch's pointed jester's cap jangled in time with his step. He carried a heavy fire iron. His face was painted with two bright red circles on his cheeks, his eyes circled with black and blue, his scarlet lips an upturned razor's slash.

The man beside him was dressed as Judy and carried a besom, his other hand held up a trailing skirt. Long black lines beamed outwards from his eyes, mimicking eyelashes. The same rosy cheeks as Punch, his thick black beard turned the painted red lips into a sucking wound.

Turnip Head's face couldn't be seen beneath his mask. The skin of a dried old hollowed out Halloween turnip lantern, wizened, lumpen and lichened, stretched round his head, tied at the back with baling twine. His features were the stuff of nightmares. A living, long-dead bog mummy. Long, coarse black hair spilled out through the twine. His eyes were empty black pits. Coal dust and charcoal covered his bare arms and shoulders. He wore an old sack over his upper body with slits for arms, and led the Horse.

This fearsome beast's skull gleamed white, its gemstone eyes glittering in the weak moonlight. Its necklace was of dried flowers. The bottom of Horse's sackcloth shroud was filthy from road dirt and showed two booted feet underneath.

They rounded a corner. The light ahead brightened as they approached a high brick wall and a set of double gates. Beyond that was the outline of a large old-stone house with a sweeping gravel drive in front, the surrounding wildness tamed into manicured lawns and neat flowerbeds. The residence radiated wealth, ease, exclusivity and superiority. A warm interior glow spilled out from its windows and shutters. Its occupants had settled in for the night, the winter. Hibernating.

The four paused before the gates, sharing a look. Again, no words needed. They nodded. The Horse threw back its skullhead and neighed. Petals from its dead flower necklace fluttered in the air like loosed flakes of dead skin. Turnip Head pulled on the reins, calmed the Horse down.

Mr Punch pushed open a gate.

They walked up the drive.

Ready to gain admission. Sing their blood harmonies.

Nick West stared at the TV screen, pretending to watch whatever was on. He didn't see it, didn't hear it. Just shapes and colours dancing in front of his eyes. He might have been staring at concrete for all the difference it made to him.

Simon. Nick's ungrateful bastard of a son had alluded to things before, talked round them, insinuated. But never said any of it outright, to his face, to Ludmilla's face. The entitled, privileged little prick. Standing there, whining about not being able to see his mates again. But the fact was, the little brat couldn't go out until he could be trusted not to tell anyone who he was and why he was there.

Nick had replied with his hey I'm-your-dad-everything's-going-to-be-OK voice. Come on, mate, that's a bit harsh. You know why we're here, why we have to keep quiet for a while, start again. Look, Angelica's managing, why couldn't Simon? And his son's reply? Because when she starts moaning on, you buy her something to shut her up. When Simon said that, Angelica had almost glanced up from her iPhone that Nick had bought her. Almost. It had taken his all, but Nick remained calm. Look, mate, we all have to make sacrifices. We pull together, like families do. Simon's reply?

Tell that to Mum.

Nick had reddened at the words, hitting him with the force of a slap to the face.

Tell that to Mum.

Ludmilla had stepped forward, started to tell both Nick and Simon what she thought of them both. Simon didn't give her the chance. He started straight in on her, calling her all sorts of horrible names he'd clearly been saving up. Eventually, with no words left, he'd stomped upstairs, Nick shouting after him. Ludmilla had tried to vent her anger on Nick, but for once he wouldn't let her. After his halfhearted defense of his son, he retreated to the lounge, fell into the armchair, and stared at the TV.

That ungrateful little shit. After everything Nick had done for him. OK, yes, maybe there had been a little bit of overlap between starting to see Ludmilla and ending it with Claire. But Claire was in a hospice, the cancer wasn't getting any better, she wasn't going be around for much longer, so what was he supposed to do? No one could blame him. Not really. Nick had desperately needed someone to hold, to look after him. Someone who showed him love. Ludmilla had done that, all right. So, yes, maybe their coming together had been a bit unconventional, but one way of looking at it was that Nick had rescued Ludmilla from a horrible future. He was her knight in shining armour. Surely that counted for something?

Yes, Ludmilla would have preferred his kids not to live with them, but what could Nick do? They had to go somewhere, and it wouldn't be forever, he'd assured her. Boarding schools, and that. Then this happened and they had to make the big move. The four of them ended up stuck with each other, whether they liked it or not.

But that didn't excuse Simon's awful behaviour. Nick should not have to put up with that, and he wasn't prepared to. Even in this house, under these conditions.

Just let him say something more. Just let him try again and see what he gets. He'll—

The doorbell rang.

'What the f*** is this now?'

Nick carried over his anger, yanked open the door.

He jumped. There were four of them.

The big bloke looked like he had some advanced and terminal skin disease, but Nick quickly realized it was just a mask. His bare arms were muscled, hairy, and seemingly impervious to the cold. He wore an old sack, and he held a decorated horseskull on a rope. The horse costume had someone beneath it, wrapped in a sheet and operating the jaw. Like a ghost horse in a cheap pantomime.

And the other two were, if anything, even odder. Two men dressed like Punch and Judy, their faces garishly made up. Judy had a beard. Punch held a large metal poker, Judy a witch's broom constructed with a wooden tree-limb handle and bristles of twigs. Punch, Judy and the big one with the rotting face and the wild hair were all in soot, like they'd just emerged from down a pit.

'We have to sing to be allowed entrance,' said Punch, his voice as bizarre as his puppet show counterpart.

'You're not coming in here.'

Punch grinned. It split his bright red lips like a knife across a throat. 'Yes, we are. We sing, you battle us in song and rhyme. You admit defeat. Then we enter and entertain you.'

Before Nick could reply, Judy, in a high, strained voice at odds with the bearded face, started singing: 'Bright sun, dark death, lord of the winds, lord of the dance—'

'Right, just shut up and leave now.' Nick tried to close the door, but the big, masked guy wedged his booted foot in the doorway. Punch slowly shook his head. Judy continued the song.

'Sun child and winter-born king, hanged one, untamed, untamed, stag and stallion, goat and bull, sailor of the last sea, guardian of the gate, brother and lover—'

'Stop it!' shouted Nick. 'Stop it!'

His cries brought Ludmilla to the door. 'What is this?'

Nick turned to her helplessly while the song continued.

'They just…they won't go away.'

'Seed sower, grain reborn, come horned one…'

Ludmilla yanked the door wide open. 'Leave here. Now.'

'Our song has ended,' said Punch. 'Now it's your turn.'

'Leave,' said Ludmilla once more, in a voice that usually had others cowering. 'Now.'

The four looked at each other and quickly arrived at a decision. Punch said, 'We win.'

He pushed his way inside the open door. The others followed.

'You can't, just, please…' Nick flapped impotently around them as the four strode into the grand house like they owned the place. Ludmilla looked between her ineffectual husband and the intruders, following them into the living room. *EastEnders* still played in the background. Angelica looked up from her phone, eyes widening. She didn't move.

Punch moved over to the fireplace. 'Let the battle of poetry and song commence…'

Nick ran up to him. 'Look, just who are you? What d'you want?'

Punch squared up to him, staring him in the face. Something unpleasant danced behind his eyes. 'It's tradition. You of all people should know that. You've even got a traditional name. Nicholas. Nick. Saint Nick,' he said, his voice sing-song. He leaned in closer. An unpleasant odour that Nick couldn't identify emanated from him. 'But you're no saint, are you, Nick?' He stretched the name out slowly.

'What—? How do you know my name?' Nick looked around, his anger giving way to fear. 'Who are you?'

'Just locals, welcoming the incomers. Traditional, this time of year.'

Before anyone else could speak or move, the Horse started whinnying and neighing. Rearing its head up, shaking the desiccated decorations around its neck, ringing its bells. In its eye sockets were what looked like two green-glass bottle bottoms. Reflecting light made jewels of them. The Horse snapped its skeletal jaws, ducking and diving as the person underneath maneuvered. The masked man holding the rein made a faint pretense of trying to tame the wayward creature.

'*Whoa* there,' he said as uninterestedly as possible – an actor chosen for his physique not his ability.

The Horse, as seemed to be the plan, ignored his handler. He dropped the rein, and the Horse cavorted around the living room, weaving its way between pieces of furniture, stopping to stare and snap at

Angelica, putting its bony snout right in her face.

She screamed, screwed her eyes tight shut, tried to curl up inside herself. Even Ludmilla, famous for her fearsome temper, cowered in the corner.

'What are you doing?' shouted Nick. 'Why are you doing this? Please leave. Now.'

They ignored him. Judy began sweeping the rug with the witch's broom. Punch opened the wood burner and poked at the fire inside. The Horse kept galloping. The one with the rotted face just watched.

'You shouldn't let us do this,' said Punch, hitting burning logs with his poker, sounding even more like the seaside puppet he was trying to be come to life. 'You shouldn't let me rake out the fire. When it's gone, it's gone.'

Nick didn't know what that meant, but it didn't sound good.

'I'm phoning the police.' He grabbed Angelica's mobile, but the masked man suddenly came to life. He was surprisingly quick; grabbing the phone from Nick's hand, crushing his fingers in the process. He threw the device into the wood burner where Punch hit it with the poker.

'Naughty phone! Naughty phone! Can't have that, can we?' Punch smashed it into hot little pieces. 'Can't have our festive fun spoiled.'

Angelica curled into a foetal ball, arms covering her head. Whimpering.

'What do you want?' Nick screamed as hard as he could, terrified.

Punch straightened up. Stared at him.

'Don't you know?'

'No.'

'Guess.'

A realization dawned on Nick's face.

'No…'

Punch smiled before addressing his comrades: 'Search the house.'

Extract from *Gravedigger's Song*,
Martyn Waites, Blackstone Publishing, 2022,
reprinted with permission of the author.

#eatdrinkrelax

JOLYON TUCK

There's enough light still to see the colours of the hanging baskets along the river. The reds, yellows, purples and blues are all greying in the half-light of the evening. They sag and look like they have seen better days. They look thirsty. I know how they feel.

A glass of lager is brought to me by a man in a hooped T-shirt, the style once associated with the garlic sellers cycling around the heads of an Englishman's perception of France. These days it has become the uniform for ladies over sixty, so to see it here, on a man no older than twenty-five years seems slightly jarring. He wears an orange apron of a good solid material, and as he places the glass before me on the picnic table I can't help but think it would be better suited to a butcher than a barman.

He turns over a metal dish on the table and reveals it as an ashtray. The implication is that if I want to enjoy the fresh air of the quayside on a summer evening, I had better be there to smoke.

There is a pot on the table, containing a small rosemary plant. The barman's final act of service to me is to take this pot away. At first I think this is a reflection of how my expected smoking would damage the plant, and then I become more concerned that his removal of the plant might have flagged me up as a non-smoker, and trouble might soon follow. It is only when he begins collecting the plants from the neighbouring tables that I notice each pot has a number painted on the side. His collecting the table numbers is, of course, an indication that the pub is no longer serving food. The kitchen is now closed.

This might solve one mystery, as I am very much aware of sitting under the constant drone of an extractor fan. I have already weighed up the possibility that the noise is either from the kitchen or the toilets and, not knowing the layout of the inside of the pub, I decide not to dwell on this too much. I like to think, as a basic rule of thumb, intermittent droning is a hand dryer, constant droning is a kitchen. Whichever the case, the droning does not stop simply because the table numbers have been collected.

There is a constant flow of bubbles rising up from the middle of my glass. It's not a pint glass as I remember them. It's one of those glasses with a stem that tries to make a pint of lager classier than it really is. It pretends to be a glass of wine, but you never see people holding a pint of lager by the stem in the way they might a glass of wine. I'll hold my pint like I've always held a pint, and I'll thank you to not try and gentrify my experience.

A dogwalker passes through a small cloud of mist in the half moonlight. It looks like she's stifling a yawn, but there's a tiny metal device in her hand, and another cloud of mist appears around her. I realise this is exactly what I need, a stealth vape, something to hold up to my face. It's a poor substitute for the real thing, but it would help me get through the next few minutes. She takes the path down the riverside that leads to the bridge, leaving her light fruity mist behind.

I can see the bridge from here, suspended like a dark frown, showing nothing but disdain for the water beneath and the people daring to make use of it at this hour. There is a couple on the bridge, looking down at the river. He's holding her from behind and pointing. The surface of the river may well be rippling, but there's no reflection of the moon from where I sit. At best, he must be pointing to the reflection of a seagull circling above, at the boats moored up on the riverside or pointing out where she'll end up if she dares to cross him again.

There's music. It's not coming from my pub. I'd not visit anywhere with enforced entertainment. I'll take the grumbling of an extractor fan over a live singer any day. It's either travelling up from one of the bars further down my side of the river or worse, it may be coming across from the restaurants on the other side. I don't care where it's coming from, I just want it to stop.

There's a sign outside my venue. 'Independent,' it says. 'Proper pub. Warm welcome.' Proper pub, eh? Beer brought in glasses with stems by men dressed as French butchers?

The sign says, '#eatdrinkrelax.'

What sort of proper pub uses an octothorpe?

The kitchen is closed so I won't #eat, I'm sitting at a smoking table trying not to smoke, so I can't #relax, it looks like the best I'm going to manage is to #drink.

As it gets darker I'm conscious that there are lampposts all the way down the cobbled path that lines the riverside, but they offer no light at all. It's not that they're those modern low-energy bulbs that take ages to warm up, although they probably are. It's that they're just not on.

My attention is drawn back to the river by a sound. I can only describe it as a splash. Like something has fallen from the bridge.

A lone man crosses to the far side and is walking away.

I strain to see if it is the man from the couple who had been pointing at the river minutes before. The light is so poor I can't be sure. But it can't be. I mean, somebody would notice, if you dumped a body from the bridge into the river, wouldn't they?

If I were going to dump a body, I would do it further down the river. I wouldn't do it here. This is where you come to #eatdrinkrelax.

There is rippling on the surface of the river.
I can now see the reflection of the moon.
The light of the bulb in the lamppost is warming up.
Just as I thought, a modern bulb on a timer.
It must be nine o'clock.

Trespassers Will Be Prosecuted

SARAH FOX

The rainwater seeped into the hems of Heather's pyjama trousers as she trudged down the gangway, her unlaced trainers slopping as she went. The moisture glued the freezing cold fabric to her ankles. If only she'd thrown on more than just her coat. So much for the cosy night in she had planned. Blankets, a hot water bottle and a glass of pinot while watching *Married at First Sight* in the glow of candlelight. Instead, she was out in the elements, patrolling Seacombe Harbour – her little empire on the South Devon coast.

She aimed her torch forwards. The rain fell diagonally, thrumming on the canvas rooftops of hibernating boats. Sunny-Jim, Becky Blue and Scallywag. All present and correct. The harbour was quiet this time of year. There were no tourists asking questions about mooring charges. No idiots ignoring tide times and getting into trouble. Most of the boats belonged to the locals and they knew better than to be out on a night like this. But she couldn't deny the bang. It had been substantial. Enough to drag her out of the warm cocoon of the harbour master's office.

She adjusted the peaked hood of her waterproof,

pulling it further over her face. It was ridiculous, the coat itself identified her but what else could she do? It was her duty to investigate. Technically she wasn't *on* duty but squatting in the harbour master's office for the past three nights had propelled her into overtime territory. Thank goodness nobody had discovered her sleeping bag amongst the life jackets yet.

A glimmer of light caught her attention. It jittered like a firefly from further down the pontoon.

'Damn,' she whispered in a haze of breath.

She was hoping that the noise she'd heard was just a figment of her imagination, brought into reality by her current state of unease. Heather stood still, watching as the light ahead bobbed like a sparkler on bonfire night. She dipped her torch to the ground, not wanting to draw attention to herself. Whoever it was might not have noticed her yet. She could retrace her steps, bound back up the gangway and be back under her blankets in less than five minutes.

But what if something was going on? Winter might be quiet but that never stopped the threat of opportune thieves trying their luck on the dormant vessels. She was duty bound to continue, wasn't she? Her reluctant feet stepped forward once again. She hoped it was kids. There was a chance she could overcome a tearaway teenager: startle them with her authority and send them running.

Her chest tightened along with her grip on the

torch. In the chilly night, her body tingled with heat. Confrontation was not her best skill. Especially when half-dressed in sopping wet nightwear. What if they reported her? Turned the tables. She shouldn't be here either.

Her heart pounded as she moved closer to the flickering light. She was aware of her laces. The plastic ends rattled against the meshwork like tin cans on a wedding car. To her, it was too loud, but she was too far forward to run for safety. In a moment of clarity, she clicked off her torch. Her breath quickened in the darkness as her muscle memory drove her along the familiar path. Water swayed beneath her, sloshing against the sides of the boats.

A figure emerged, tall and broad shouldered. They moved quickly, up and down, as if stacking shelves in a supermarket.

Heather glanced across the water. Her small harbour was otherwise empty. No passing traffic on the distant road. No dogs on late-night walks with disgruntled owners. She was wet, cold and on her own.

'Stop,' Heather yelled, flicking her torch back on and summoning an authority she didn't quite believe in.

The firefly stopped and turned, dazzling her with light. Her vision danced with spots. There was a bang of a door. Something tipped over. The light turned briefly away. Heather blinked, trying to readjust her sight.

'Stop,' she cried out again, her conviction withering to a squeak.

The figure moved forward, blinding her again. They leapt from the edge of the boat onto the platform. The suspended pathway clattered with the impact. Heather stepped backwards. Her sodden coat was a suffocating weight on her shoulders. Her breaths were laboured but she needed to retreat. She stumbled to the edge, dropping her torch.

Hands came from the darkness, grabbing her arms. They pulled her forwards. The hold was strong. Painful. Her shoe splashed into oblivion. The stench of fish guts filled her nostrils. Her breath caught in her throat. She scrabbled against the figure, her arms pushing against his torso. Her eyes squinted in the burning light.

'Heather?'

The grip eased.

Heather halted her flailing arms.

'Jake?' Her muscles relaxed. The relief was euphoric. Jake wasn't a thief. Jake was a mate. Once. Heather looked behind him. The boat was still in shadow.

'That's not your boat,' she said, 'You don't have a boat in my harbour.'

'Just a bit of fishing,' Jake said.

Jake knew the coastline better than she did. If he wanted to fish, he would go out to sea or cast off the beach, not fling his line off the side of the harbour.

'Are you wearing pyjamas?' he said, aiming his head torch down.

'Whose code did you use to enter the harbour? Is someone else with you?' Heather would not be deflected.

'It's chucking it down. Look at your feet. You've only got one shoe on. You must be frozen,' he said. Amusement filled his face, 'Why are you in your pyjamas?'

She would not give Jake the satisfaction of knowing her secrets. Sharing her life with him was a mistake she was not likely to make again.

A shriek pierced through their stand-off.

Heather's eyes widened.

'Who's there?' she snarled.

'Nobody.' His denial came too quick.

Heather shot past him, grabbing her torch from the floor. She aimed it towards the vessel. Its blue and yellow woodwork now visible within the beam. If he was hiding something, then she would have the ammunition she needed to keep him quiet. The last thing she wanted was him spouting off in the pub about tonight's escapades. She'd worked hard to get where she was: first female harbour master in Seacombe's history.

A girl was leaning over the far side of the boat. Her scream had given way to a guttural retch.

'Hello?' Heather said, softening her tone.

The girl slowly lifted her head. Her hair straddled her face, held in place by a mixture of rain and vomit. She had no coat, and the rain pelted her bare skin, making her skimpy dress almost see through. Heather glanced back to Jake. Fishing was obviously the last thing on his mind.

'In – the – water,' the girl stuttered. Her index finger pointed over the side of the boat, shaking frantically in mid-air. 'In the water,' she said again, this time her words were stronger, almost aggressive.

'What about the water?' Heather matched the girl's tone. She was running out of patience.

'There's a body in the water!'

FIONA MOUNTAIN

SHORT COURSE TUTOR, OCTOBER 2022

Fiona has written six novels, which have been published around the world, including America, Canada, Australia, Italy, Germany, Holland, Japan and Thailand. Fiona's first novel, *Isabella*, tells the haunting love story of Bounty mutineer Fletcher Christian and his cousin, Isabella Curwen, and was shortlisted for the Romantic Novel of the Year Award. It was followed with *Pale as the Dead* and *Bloodline*, which combine history with mystery and feature 'ancestor detective' Natasha Blake. *Bloodline* is the winner of the prestigious Mary Higgins Clark Award from the Mystery Writers of America. It has also been optioned by Leonard Goldberg (producer of TV classics such as *Charlie's Angels* and *Starsky and Hutch*). Fiona grew up in Sheffield and moved to London, aged eighteen, where she worked for the BBC, in the press office for Radio 1. She lives in the Cotswolds with her family.

In October and November 2022 Fiona taught a short course on writing historical fiction at Quay Words. Of those who took part, she has chosen Jason Mann as her *Quay Voice*.

Bloodline

FIONA MOUNTAIN

The abbreviation, *SUS*, next to an entry in the criminal records, was short for the Latin *suspendatur*, meaning, 'Let him be hanged'. It never failed to make Natasha Blake break out in goose bumps.

She'd been a genealogist for over a quarter of her twenty-nine year existence, since she graduated eight years ago, and she'd been coming to the National Archives, what used to be the less grandly titled Public Records Office, in Kew at least once a month since then.

Let him be hanged. Him was a her, in this particular instance.

Alice Hellier was just a parlour maid from Fulbrook, Oxfordshire, until she became a murderess at the age of nineteen, when she shot her sixty-four year-old employer, Samuel Purrington, on 11 August 1852. A bona fide black sheep to add a splash of colour to the rather humdrum family tree Natasha had spent the past month and a half researching.

What had led her here was a small paragraph she'd stumbled across in the *Oxfordshire Gazette* of August 1853, at the start of Alice's trial. The headline 'MURDEROUS MAID' had been enough to get her going. Now she had come for the official proof. She went over to a computer terminal, keyed in her reader number and searched the online catalogue to order the *Burford Gaol Book*, which she'd collect downstairs.

This was the type of history she loved best, the reason she did this job. Kings and Queens, famous explorers and military heroes were all very interesting, but what gave her the best buzz were people like Alice. People on whom the spotlight of history shone very faintly and just for a millisecond. Those whose names were recorded in a few dry and dusty old papers that only saw the light of day when someone summoned them from the vaults to touch them with white-gloved hands.

A few minutes later the gaol book was waiting for her at the document collections counter. Impatience kicking in, she found the entry on the way back to her allotted desk.

A whole page was devoted to Alice. In the history of lowly people like her, it was infamy that gave you your fifteen minutes of fame. If you lived a blame-free existence, the odds were that all but your vital statistics – name, dates, address and trade – were lost to future generations. Little of your essence remained. But a brush with the law left a stain that lingered as long as archives were preserved. Natasha often debated committing a crime of passion or staging a heist in an antique arcade, something to create enough intrigue for any family historians who might follow in her footsteps.

Fixed to the centre of the page was a sepia mug shot of Alice. She sat demurely with her hands clasped in her lap, a dark cape around her shoulders, her hair parted in the middle and drawn back from a solemn but pretty, round little face. She looked a lot more like a parlour maid than a murderess.

Natasha added the information to the notes she'd already made on Alice's descendants.

Her baby son, Thomas, was cared for by Alice's aunt after Alice was hanged, and, at the age of thirteen, he would be sentenced to twenty-one days' hard labour for larceny. His previous crimes were listed as arson, setting fire to a stack of wheat, night poaching. By the time he was thirty he had a wife and two children and had served two years in prison for robbery with assault. His son Jack went the same way, sentenced to one month's hard labour for stealing a pair of boots and five years in reformatory school. A bad lot, the Helliers. They came good in the end though. Jack's son became a blacksmith and his son a farmer.

She glanced out of the angled plate glass window. Flaming June, the sun Mediterranean-bright but everything still fresh and green. She hadn't minded the early start this morning, walking across the dewy Cotswold fields with her Red Setter, Boris, at six-thirty so she could catch the seven-fifteen train from

Moreton-in-Marsh, with about two seconds to spare thanks to the Sunbeam Alpine. Her beautiful old car relied on its beauty to excuse its refusal to start just when she needed it most.

It was her third trip to London in the last seven days. She'd never worked so hard as she had for the past weeks, or earned as much money in so short a time. Bloody hell, had she earned it. It was no easy task to compile a comprehensive genealogical chart going back eight generations, to 1750 to be exact, in just thirty-five days.

The precise cut-off point had been imposed by her client, Charles Seagrove, who'd also, mysteriously, demanded confidentiality so complete she wasn't even allowed to tell anyone who she was working for. Why the great secrecy? And why, when Seagrove had gone to some lengths to impress on her that he was a proficient genealogist who'd worked for Debrett's, had he employed her to do this research instead of doing it himself? While she was at it, she'd also like to know why he was so interested in the family of the person at the top of the chart, John Hellier, now aged twenty-one? Why the need for so much detail and all this great hurry to unearth the Hellier roots? Either Charles Seagrove liked to be thorough, or there was something important at stake.

Too much work, not enough play and even less sleep – she was breaking all the rules the trusty Internet

Doctor offered on how to beat insomnia. No mentally taxing activities late at night, minimize stress, don't take your work to bed with you. She knew what she was supposed to do but doing it was a different matter. Since she and Marcus had split up eighteen months ago, she'd become more a workaholic than ever. She'd had her laptop plugged into the socket by her bedside table, had been up until the early hours trawling online databases after long days at the Family Records Centre, ploughing through census returns and wills, the trade directories of the Society of Genealogists, coroners' inquests, deeds, old newspapers. She'd practically taken up residence here in the Reading Room and she'd lost count of the numbers of documents she'd requested to view. Military service records, apprenticeship books, correspondence of the Lunacy Commission, calendars of prisoners. She'd spent nearly a whole week, all in all, in the Wellcome Library for the History of Medicine, sifting through clinical and patient records, the first time she'd been asked to do that as part of genealogical research.

Hellier, if not as common as Smith or Jones, was not a rare surname, and, as usual, each line of inquiry had thrown up several possibilities. There were rather more question marks in the Hellier genealogical chart than Natasha's professionalism and perfectionism usually allowed, but that was deadlines for you and time was up. She'd done all she could. But that didn't stop her itching to go back to the contemporary local newspapers, to try to find the original news account of the murder, with the inevitable speculation on the motive, and the trial reports.

Extract from *Bloodline*,
Fiona Mountain, Orion, 2004,
reprinted with permission of the author.

Hidden Depths

JASON MANN

Extract from the final chapter of the 'wild swimming' thriller Hidden Depths *that tells the story of Cornish wife and mother Catherine Carlyon who is forced into a desperate plan to fake her own death.*

I stand in chest-deep water on a narrow, gently shelving beach of bone-white sand, staring out at the great ocean. My stomach churns at the towering prospect of the challenge I have set myself. The cold seeps into my wetsuit as I take a few gulps of an energy drink and press #1 on my GPS navigation device.

I'm ready. Or as ready as I could ever be. The countless hours of training, of relentless lengths of Satan's Pool, have built my mental as well as physical resilience.

I take a deep breath and start swimming, heading away from the Isles of Scilly, away from my old life. The first stroke is completed in a second. It carries me almost two metres. It's followed by another. And another. And another. I search for a strong, steady rhythm, focusing on each phase of the stroke.

Reach. Catch. Pull. Push.

The early minutes drag. I shrug and shake my right shoulder in the hope of clearing a persistent twinge.

On the horizon, a band of grey provides the first hint of dawn. But when I stare down into the depths of the ocean all I can see is blackness, total and complete. An LED display in my goggles, linked to the GPS, provides a reassuring green light. Green is good. It means I'm on course.

I slide past the final headland to head north-east out into the open ocean through ripples summoned by a gentle breeze. The wind is coming from behind. I like to think that it's pushing me forward, helping me on my way, that the hand of fate is guiding me, but it's merely the prevailing wind and so to be expected. Also expected is the tide which will be against me for the first few hours but then turn in my favour.

My body warms to the task. The ache in my shoulder fades, the stroke becomes easier, more fluid. As I push on ever further into the immensity of the open ocean, the pale grey to my right brightens until replaced by the first blinding shards of daylight. Sunlight brings a growing optimism. The impossible seems possible.

I take a break, treading water while drinking sparingly from a container of energy drink. Dehydration is only one of the enemies I'll face over the coming hours. I have three litres, held in a belt and a swim buoy tethered to me by a short line. It's barely enough. Usually, I'd expect to drink more than twice as much.

I can't resist looking back the way I have come. The Isles of Scilly have shrunk to a series of flat rocks on the horizon. If there was a time to turn around, it would be now. I could freestyle my way back to the isles and slip ashore on the beach where I started with nobody noticing my absence.

But there can be no going back.

A few days ago, a foggy moor felt like the loneliest place on earth, but it is as nothing compared with being out here, with so far to go and so much fatigue to come. There is nobody to shout encouragement, no welcoming hands to reach down and pluck me to safety.

I press on. Beyond the point of no return. I will reach Cornwall or I will die. Nothing could be simpler or more clear-cut. If I fail, my remains will become part of the great cycle of sea life, absorbed in the guts of sleek creatures riding the waves. For me, a child of the ocean, such an end is not so terrible.

I learned long ago to focus on each small step rather than the total task, the enormity of which will invite despair. How do you climb a mountain? One step at a time. How do I conquer this enormous churning expanse? One stroke at a time.

The directional light in my goggles winks amber. I'm off course. A correction is needed. A miniscule adjustment in my bearing is rewarded by a green light.

At last, the tide turns to help me. My adrenaline-fuelled body is strong. As the sun rises, the colour of the ocean below changes from pure black to emerald green. I gaze down to see shafts of sunlight lancing down into its crystal-clear depths. It's astoundingly beautiful. And yet sinister. It is here that the lost kingdom of Lyonesse was swallowed by the ocean in a single night. Far below me in the chill void, grotesque creatures gobble, writhe and squirm. I imagine the huge maw of a shark, filled with razor sharp teeth, rising from the depths.

Legends and fears of sea monsters are for children – and ancient mariners. I banish them and immerse myself in the mechanics of swimming, making my stroke as efficient as possible. If I can complete enough strokes, I will succeed, will survive. During those long, lonely hours, my roaming mind plays with the arithmetic of the swim, the humbling distances and the superhuman effort needed. Twenty-eight miles. At least fifteen hours. About 12,000 turns of each arm and as many life-giving breaths. More than 100,000 thumping heartbeats.

Reach. Catch. Pull. Push.

One more completed. Another tiny piece in the jigsaw slotted into place. I breathe to my left, only switching to my right when my neck aches in protest at the repetition. My focus is on getting to the hourly feed stop. The sweet energy drink and jelly babies are a small reward I can look forward to. But I keep each stop to no more than two or three minutes. If I halt for too long my muscles will chill and it will be hard to get going again.

One swimming hour slides into the next and then the next. My mind wanders. I lose myself in the surge and swell of my environment. The Isles of Scilly have long since sunk below the horizon. There is only endless ocean ahead and behind, impenetrable depths below and a pale sky with wispy cloud above. I am lost in the immensity of it all, feeling minute and inconsequential, a speck in the great cosmos.

And then, in the far-off haze, the first smudge of land. When I catch sight of the cliffs at Land's End my adrenaline surges and I raise my stroke rate. The finish is in sight.

But it's a cruel deception. I'm barely halfway. As time grinds onwards, the mainland seems as distant as ever. My pace slows again. I force myself to stop looking ahead, instead concentrating on the little things – the swirl of the cool water through my hands, the sparkling bubbles which burst from my mouth and trail from my fingertips, the beauty of the stroke.

CLAIRE WILCOX

GUEST WRITER, MARCH 2023

Claire Wilcox is Professor in Fashion Curation at London College of Fashion and was Senior Curator of Fashion at the V&A, where she curated many exhibitions, including co-curating *Frida Kahlo: Making Her Self Up* (2018). She instigated Fashion in Motion (live catwalk events in the Museum, 1999–present) and was Lead Curator for the refurbishment and redisplay of the V&A's Fashion Gallery in 2012. She has authored numerous publications and in 2021 won the PEN Ackerley Prize for Biography for her memoir *Patch Work: A Life Amongst Clothes* (2020).

In March 2023 we welcomed Claire to Quay Words to discuss her memoir during our 'Threads' season, which delved into text and the textile, pulling at the threads of Exeter Custom House's history of the fabric trade. In *Patch Work* we see through the eyes of a curator how the stories and secrets of clothes measure out the passage of time, our gains and losses, and the way we use them to unravel and write our histories.

Patch Work

Imprint

CLAIRE WILCOX

For Circe Henestrosa and Gannit Ankori.

The medical bandages were dipped in buckets of plaster and wrapped around her naked torso in layers which gradually hardened to provide a rigid carapace, immobilising any movement that would undo the benefits of the surgery on her vertebrae and thus cause further damage to her spine; and all the while the young woman – only nineteen – hung by her feet while the plaster was dried with blasts of hot air, so that the bespoke corset – which she would wear for weeks, if not months – would hold true. And once, when this performance was conducted at her family home on the corner of Allende and Calle Londres, the bandages were wrapped too tightly, and as they heated and contracted – as plaster will do in exothermic reaction when mixed with water – the girdle began to compress her lungs and, terrified by her screaming, her family had to cut her free from its grip without recourse to medical shears, for the doctor had left and there was no orthopaedic cast technician with an oscillating cast saw to hand, for it was the 1920s.

These stories Frida Kahlo told about herself with gusto and humour, never self-pity, just as she told many other stories, firstly about the childhood polio that led to a weakened and shorter right leg and how she was teased for this, and then the near-fatal accident that compounded this imbalance and added many more troubles to her stoic body. Her subsequent suffering and the endless ways she tried to be cured of an injury that could not be cured, at least not at that time, when such operations – and she had many – were likely to do as much harm as good, meant that she was often bed-bound, and here she held court, much in the manner of a queen receiving guests in her bedchamber.

The corsets – there were others, some made of leather, some in the form of back braces ordered in America, where she also sought medical help – imbued her with a stiff, regal posture, and you see this in her demeanour, over and again. In her self-portrait *Me and My Doll* (1937) we see her sitting upright on a rush-based, simple wooden bed on a terracotta-tiled floor. She is dressed in a long green skirt with frothy white flounce that hides her legs and a loose blouse with a band of red embroidery around the neck, and she holds a cigarette – her ubiquitous attendant, counterbalance to the artist's brush. A large, undressed doll (she liked to dress and undress her dolls) with porcelain-white skin – in contrast to her own – sits beside her like a phantom child. But look closer, for the initial impression of tranquillity and innocence is disrupted by the fact it has a damaged foot, in wry acknowledgement of her own.

In the photographs, of which there are many – for Kahlo had a magnetically compelling visage and an ability to look straight through the camera to the viewer's eye – it is evident that she was a gift for photographers, including her father, who documented his favourite daughter throughout her childhood and early adulthood with the careful objectivity of love, and her lover, Nikolas Muray, whose technically magnificent colour carbro portraits made us fall for her too. Here she is in a picture by one of the leading art photographers of the day, Edward Weston, in San Francisco in the early 1930s, newly arrived; on the cusp of becoming herself. She is wearing a fringed shawl and the weight of her country's history in the form of a triple string of heavy, pre-Hispanic jade beads unearthed from graves: single beads once placed in the mouths of the dead, strung together to encircle her stalk of a neck.

Many years later, our conservator finds touches of green paint on the necklace, as if a brush has been held against it to match their hue; these very beads can be seen in several of the self-portraits and were buried for a second time, in a locked bathroom for half a century after her death, alongside most of her personal possessions, and only discovered a decade or so ago.

Many women photographed Kahlo too, for the development of hand-held Leicas and Kodaks unarguably allowed physical and artistic liberation, as reportage journalism became a profession that was, uniquely, open to women, who were able to traverse diverse political terrains under official protection as news gatherers and image collectors of the artistic milieu of their time. I list them: Tina Modotti, her revolutionary friend and artist; the French-German photojournalist Gisèle Freund; her compatriot and friend, Lola Álvarez Bravo. They sought her at home, mostly; in her bed, in her garden, camera-ready, dressed as if for a carnival, regarding herself in one of the many mirrors that filled her house, offering a kaleidoscopic multiplicity of images that, patched together, in the end, conceal as much as they reveal, for she is always in control. Perhaps her true self can only be seen through the mirror, so important for the self-portraitist; one was even set into the canopy of her sickbed by her parents so she could see, and paint, herself. And all the while that she is standing, sitting, lying, we witness this regal nature that was a combination of physical injury and powerful, charismatic personality and *difference*.

The differentiation between herself and others was epitomised by a colourful and dignified way of dressing that eschewed fashion and convention, down to her black bird-wing eyebrows and sable-soft moustache, that drew on the regional clothing and textile traditions of Puebla and Tehuantepec and other regions but that was – and there is no other word for it – mixed up with vintage. This took the form of skirts cut from the silk of nineteenth-century gowns, shawls from the same century, American thrift-store blouses, jangling jewellery of little or no value (except for the heavy gold dowry necklaces sourced from the Isthmus of Tehuantepec). She wore her long skirts with under-petticoats and flounces (removable, for laundering) that swept the floor, and stitched bells onto them so that people could hear her coming; and her embroidered blouses were loose fitting, in the traditional way, hence without fastenings, for they were simple lengths of textile seamed at either side with a hole left for the arms and another for the neck (such garments can be quickly folded up and put away, and take up no hanger space), and these could be easily pulled on and off, for someone who had to wear a corset. And these plaster corsets, with their solid porous surfaces, were like frescoes on which she could paint, so that she was wearing another layer, body art if you like, bearing her own brushwork – a act of bravado to decorate one's tormentor as if, as my curator friend said, she had *explicitly chosen to wear them*.

The corsets, like the paintings, are an X-ray into her pre-occupations: communism, in the form of a hammer and sickle; pain, shown as the torture of a spine depicted as a crumbling column; childlessness, for one has a delicately painted unborn child over the abdomen, the image taken from an illustrated obstetrics manual. She dealt with loss by studying it and by painting it, and in keeping with her country's close relationship with death, even kept a foetus in a jar in her bedroom, said to have been given to her by one of her surgeons. The bandages that went to make the corsets, the plaster that bore the imprint of her body, the half-shells that survive (for plaster corsets have to be cut down each side to release their occupants) reveal their internal truth to form – for example the dip to accommodate the breasts, the swelling out above the hips, the sweat. They emulate the way that a couture garment, made for a specific body, with its own internal rigidity made not from plaster but from crin and baleen and other stiffening materials, can be regarded as a body mould, a source of information from which internal dimensions can be taken so that, if needed (and it was needed, once, in the museum) a client could be identified without doubt by their torso, if one had another of their corseted garments with which to compare, and so they bear testament to the uniqueness of each body.

No one is symmetrical. I should know; scoliosis runs in the family. So, when we look inside those plaster corsets and see the faint texture of bandage and imprints of her pores in the plaster, we are also seeing the shadow of one upon whose body it was moulded; who once bore its weight. Casts and moulds, corsets and girdles, sweat and wear; asymmetry, a fragile spine. Whether medical or fashionable, what could be more intimate, especially when it protects the beating heart?

Extract from *Patch Work*, Claire Wilcox,
Bloomsbury Publishing, 2020,
reprinted with permission.

INDEX OF CONTRIBUTORS

QUAY VOICES

ALBINIA, ALICE   p13

Alice Albinia is the award-winning author of twinned works of fiction and non-fiction. She worked as an editor and journalist in Delhi, teaches and lectures in universities and schools, and has travelled all around the edges of Britain, piecing together ancient, medieval and modern myths of islands ruled by women.

AMESBURY, DAWN   p124

Yorkshirewoman Dawn Amesbury is a neuro-divergent, single parent of two. Thanks to her teen historical mystery *Village of Spies*, she has been an All Stories mentee, longlisted for the Moniack Mhor Emerging Writer Award and shortlisted for the Wells Festival of Literature Children's Novel Award. She is currently writing another top-secret teen historical mystery.

BEDFORD, CHERRY   p28

Cherry Bedford was born and raised in North Devon. She is an animal epidemiologist and a keen climber. Literature has always been a passion and an escape for Cherry, from devouring novels as a child to, more lately, writing. She is currently working on her first novel and loving every minute of the process.

BENSON, FIONA   p64

Fiona Benson's pamphlet was 'Faber New Poets 1' in the Faber New Poets series, and her full-length collection *Bright Travellers* (Cape, 2014) received the Seamus Heaney Prize for first collection and the Geoffrey Faber Memorial Prize. Her second book, *Vertigo & Ghost* (Cape, 2019) won the Roehampton Poetry Prize and the Forward Poetry Prize. Her third collection is *Ephemeron* (2022).

BOYCE-HURD, MELISSA   p119

Melissa is a writer, translator and musician who studied French at the University of Oxford and has an MA in Children's Literature Media and Culture from the University of Glasgow. At thirteen, she wrote a YA novel which was later shortlisted by Penguin Publishing for their WriteNow 2018 programme. In 2021, she wrote the script and music for a new musical called *Améliore*, which was performed at Camden Fringe.

CRAWFORD, ABBY   p32

Abby is a twenty-eight-year-old writer and poet living in Exeter. She earned her BA in English at the University of Plymouth and has a few online publications. Her poem 'Lahore 2022' recently received a commendation from the Crysse Morrison Prize for Poetry 2023.

DUMONT, SOPHIE   p142

Sophie Dumont is a poet, copywriter and ex-canoe coach living in Bristol. She is an alumna of Exeter University and her poetry has been published widely, including in *The Rialto*. Sophie won the Brian Dempsey Memorial Prize 2021, came third in the Magma Poetry Competition and has been shortlisted for the Bridport Prize twice.

ELSON JANE   p113

After performing as an actress and comedy improviser, Jane fell into writing stories and plays. Her books have won many literary awards including Peters Book of the Year two years running. Her debut novel, *A Room Full of Chocolate*, was longlisted for the Branford Boase Award and she has twice been nominated for the Carnegie Medal. Jane is loud and proud about her dyslexia and over the years has mentored many neurodiverse young people.

FOX, SARAH   p167

Sarah lives in Kingsbridge and has an MA in Creative Writing from Bath Spa University. She is currently in the process of editing her debut crime novel, *The Man on the Hill*, set in the fictional Devon town of

Seacombe. Before writing, Sarah was a paediatric nurse for twenty years.

HEADWAY, DEVON   p89
Headway Devon is an Exeter-based charity dedicated to improving life after brain injury, providing essential services across Devon and Torbay for people with acquired brain injuries, their families and carers.

JONES, LOU   p148
Lou is a wildlife gardener and wildflower grower, living near the quayside. She grew up in Exeter and, since returning to live there, has enjoyed many therapeutic moments along the riverside, observing its nature.

JOSEPH, ANTHONY   p61
Anthony Joseph is a Trinidad-born poet, novelist, academic and musician. In 2019 he was awarded a Jerwood Compton Poetry Fellowship. He is the author of five poetry collections and three novels. He lectures in creative writing at Kings College, London.

LADD, HARULA   p69
Harula is a slam-winning poet, performer and creative facilitator, with over fifteen years' experience in leading creative writing workshops. Performance highlights have included gigs with Spork!/Milk in Bristol and Hot Poets/Tongue Fu at London's Southbank Centre. Her poem 'Skin' was nominated for the Pushcart Prize in 2021.

LYONS, KAT   p64

Kat Lyons (they/them) is a queer Bristol-based writer, performer, workshop facilitator and creative producer whose work is grounded in everyday politics and a love of storytelling. They are the current Bristol City Poet (2022–2024) and were nominated for the Jerwood Poetry in Performance Award 2022. Kat's debut collection *Love Beneath the Nails* was published in February 2022 by Verve Poetry Press.

MANN, JASON   p180

Jason Mann is an award-winning journalist and writer living in Torquay. His first novel, a 'wild swimming' thriller called *Hidden Depths*, was published this year and received extensive publicity. It is available on Amazon as an ebook or paperback. His next novel *The Echoing Shore* has been longlisted for the 2023 Yeovil Literary Prize.

MENMUIR, WYL   p37

Wyl Menmuir is a novelist and editor based in Cornwall. His debut novel *The Many*, published by Salt, was longlisted for the 2016 Man Booker Prize. He teaches creative writing at Falmouth University and is a co-creator of Cornish Writing Centre, The Writers' Block.

MENDEZ, JUAN CARLOS,   p23

Juan Carlos Mendez was born in Mexico City in 1983. After completing a PhD in Neuroscience, he moved to the UK to work as a postdoctoral researcher at the University of Oxford. He is currently a Lecturer at the University of Exeter and is working on his first novel.

MILLER, ANDREW   p91

Andrew Miller, award-winning author of nine novels, was born in Bristol and studied at Middlesex Polytechnic, University of East Anglia and at Lancaster University, where he completed his PhD. He has been awarded the James Tait Black Memorial Prize, the Grinzane Cavour, the International IMPAC and the Costa Book of the Year.

MOONEY, SARAH   p106

Sarah Mooney has enjoyed being Storyteller-in-Residence for Seven Stories, the Roald Dahl Foundation, the National Portrait Gallery and SS Great Britain. She sailed across the Atlantic with an all-female crew and plays the Witch of Wookey Hole in her spare time. She has written two books and a play for children.

MOUNTAIN, FIONA   p173

Fiona's first novel, *Isabella*, was shortlisted for the Parker Romantic Novel of the Year Award. It was followed with *Pale as the Dead* and *Bloodline*, which combine history with mystery and feature 'ancestor detective', Natasha Blake. *Bloodline* is the winner of the prestigious Mary Higgins Clark Award. She lives in the Cotswolds with her family.

PARKIN, CALEB p86

Bristol City Poet 2020–2022, Caleb is an award-winning poet and tutors for the Poetry Society, Poetry School, Cheltenham Festivals and First Story. He holds an MSc in Creative Writing for Therapeutic Purposes (CWTP).

PITTS, JOHNY p57

Johny is an award-winning writer, photographer and broadcaster known for his work in exploring African–European identities. He is the author of *Afropean: Notes from Black Europe*. He collaborated with Roger Robinson on *Home Is Not A Place*, a free-form composition of photography poetry and essays in search of an answer to the question 'What is Black Britain?'

QUINLIVAN, DAVINA p50

Davina is a Lecturer in the Department of English and Creative Writing at the University of Exeter. Her memoir *Shalimar: A Story of Place and Migration* was published by Little Toller Books (2022) and she is currently writing a follow-up, *Waterlines*, on rivers and migration, trauma and healing.

RENTZENBRINK, CATHY p75

Cathy Rentzenbrink's books include *The Last Act of*

Love, *How to Feel Better* and *Dear Reader*. Her first novel is *Everyone Is Still Alive* and *Write It All Down* is a friendly and down-to-earth guide to writing a memoir. Cathy regularly chairs literary events, interviews authors, runs creative writing courses and speaks and writes on life, death, love and literature.

RESILIENT WOMEN   p73
Exeter's Resilient Women Project supports women with a range of needs including homelessness, mental health, domestic abuse and isolation. Project Manager Jeanie Lynch reports that the project supports 200 women on a regular basis.

ROBINSON, ROGER   p57
Roger is an award-winning writer and educator, chosen by Decibel as one of 50 writers who have influenced the Black British writing canon. He is the winner of the 2019 T.S. Eliot Prize and the 2020 RSL Ondaatje Prize. He collaborated with Johny Pitts on *Home Is Not A Place*, a free-form composition of photography, poetry and essays in search of an answer to the question 'What is Black Britain?'

SERGEANT, DAVID   p99
David Sergeant grew up in West Cornwall, lives in Exeter and teaches literature and creative writing at the University of Plymouth. He is the author of

several collections of poetry and is currently working on his first novel.

SHERWOOD, KIM   p44

Kim has taught at the University of Sussex, UWE, and in schools, libraries and prisons, and now lectures at the University of Edinburgh, where she lives in the city. Her first novel, *Testament*, published in 2018, won the Bath Novel Award and the *Harper's Bazaar* Big Book of the Year, was shortlisted for the Author's Club Best First Novel Award and was longlisted for the Desmond Elliott Prize.

STEPHENSON, HEIDI   p149

Heidi Stephenson is a poet-activist with a deep commitment to the earth, nonviolence and animal rights. She writes regularly for *International Times* and all-creatures.org and recently completed her first collection *WILD CRY! Vegan Verse For Planet Earth*. In 2021 she was Arts Council–funded to write her eco-poem 'The Re-Greening':http://internationaltimes.it/the-re-greening/.

STODDART, GRETA   p10

Greta Stoddart studied drama at Manchester University and acting at the École Internationale de Théâtre Jacques Lecoq in Paris. She co-founded the theatre company Brouhaha. Her first poetry collection,

At Home in the Dark (Anvil Press, 2001), won the Geoffrey Faber Memorial Prize and was shortlisted for the Forward Prize for Best First Collection. She lives in Devon.

TUCK, JOLYON   p162

Jolyon spends his days working in the criminal justice system and his nights reading as much crime fiction as he can lay his hands on. He writes for fun and acts for fun and is a law-abiding citizen (until somebody proves otherwise).

WAITES, MARTYN   p151

Martyn Waites trained at the Birmingham School of Speech and Drama and worked as an actor for many years before becoming a writer. He has been nominated for every major British crime fiction award and has enjoyed international commercial success with eight novels written under the name Tania Carver. He lives in Exeter.

WEDGWOOD CLARKE, JOHN   p83

John was born and raised in Cornwall. He trained as an actor at the Guildhall School of Music and Drama before going on to study literature and complete a PhD. He is an Associate Professor in Creative Writing at the University of Exeter.

WILCOX, CLAIRE p185

Claire was Senior Curator of Fashion at the V&A. She is Professor in Fashion Curation at the London College of Fashion. Her memoir *Patch Work: A Life Amongst Clothes* was awarded the 2021 PEN Ackerley Prize.

YOUNG VOICES

PHOTOGRAPHS

Detail from the Table of Tonnage on Vessels entering into, and of Tolls on Goods conveyed on the Exeter Canal, 1829
© Juliette Mills

Cover Image

Exeter Custom House Entrance
© Genoveva Arteaga

Inside front cover

Home Is Not A Place
© Johny Pitts

p**60**

ACKNOWLEDGEMENTS

Quay Words at Exeter Custom House is made possible by our cultural partnership with Exeter Canal and Quay Trust. We are hugely grateful for their support and their trust in Literature Works to shape, curate and deliver the literature programme. We acknowledge and thank all those who have responded to our calls for writers-in-residence, tutors, performers and masterclass leaders. Thanks also to all the new and emerging writers who took part in the programme, alongside the many who bought tickets, tuned in online, gave constructive feedback and simply helped to make Quay Words the literary lynchpin it has become.

We wish to acknowledge the support of a number of affiliates and partners who have contributed to the programme: Arvon, Devon & Exeter Institution, Exeter UNESCO City of Literature, Headway Devon, Libraries Unlimited, Resilient Women Project, Speaking Volumes, Sprung Sultan, University of Exeter, Wellcome Centre for the Cultures and Environments of Health.

We are indebted to a number of individuals who have gone out of their way to ensure the continued smooth operation of the Quay Words programme.

Grateful thanks to David Adcock and his team at Exeter Custom House, to Anna Gilroy and to Matt Newbury. Thanks are due also to Heather Holcroft-Pinn, who has brilliantly project-managed Quay Words for Literature Works since 2020.

EXETER CANAL
AND QUAY TRUST

Established in 1981, Exeter Canal and Quay Trust (ECQT) is a registered charity committed to developing Exeter Quayside as a vibrant destination for residents and visitors. It has devoted the past forty years to the conservation and regeneration of a significant portfolio of historic buildings in the Quay area. The Grade 1–listed Custom House is the trust's flagship building, which provides the perfect historic location for Quay Words. ECQT commissioned Literature Works to create and deliver the Quay Words programme, using a grant received by the trust from the Arts Council England National Lottery.

LITERATURE WORKS

Literature Works is the regional literature development agency for South West England, a registered charity and an Arts Council England National Portfolio organisation. We aim to open up the flexible literature artform of poetry and story, creative writing and reading as widely as we can to the benefit of all in the South West of England and beyond. We are committed to diversity and to the socially engaged use of literature to develop communities and support wellbeing. We nurture talent and provide resources. Our website is a dynamic and constantly updating source of information, rich with activity around the region.

BECOME A MEMBER
OF LITERATURE WORKS

The Quay Words programme continues into 2023. If you'd like to be involved, consider signing up to our free one-year Literature Works membership. Membership gives you access to priority booking and exclusive offers on a range of Quay Words author events and development opportunities for writers.

Sign up today at
www.literatureworks.org.uk/membership

You can view and get involved
in the Quay Words programme at
www.quaywords.org.uk